Untangling the Web

Applications of the Internet and Other Information Technologies to Higher Learning

David J. McArthur
Matthew W. Lewis

RAND Education

RAND

PREFACE

In just a couple of years, the Internet and World Wide Web have transformed communication, scholarship, and business. But what potential do they hold for changing higher education—the place where this technology, once called the ARPANET, originated over twenty years ago? Will they help universities reduce costs in the face of often-dramatic budget reductions? Will distance learning (dissemination of educational material and information through electronic and hardcopy media, rather than face-to-face), digital libraries, and new "virtual universities" make education available to students cheaply, and at any place or time? Or might the Web threaten higher education more than save it? Will nimble for-profit providers, who now increasingly use the Internet to deliver corporate training, soon turn to the education market and compete with traditional colleges and universities? If so, how might higher-education institutions respond to this challenge? How will they acquire the hardware and software needed to offer high-quality educational services at prices they can afford? And how can faculty quickly adapt to styles of teaching and learning that, for example, emphasize interactive mentoring instead of traditional lectures?

This report is the product of a small RAND study that attempted to frame and develop some answers to these questions. It is intended both as a broad review of ongoing and planned applications of the Internet and Web in higher education, and as an analysis of key technical and educational issues—as well as broader social issues—that these applications highlight. We hope that this report will stimulate discussions regarding the costs and benefits of Web technologies in learning, the different models these technologies offer for providing education, and the changing relationships between traditional institutions of higher education and a new generation of providers.

This paper was completed in fall of 1996 (with minor updates prior to official RAND publication in early 1998) and reflects the state of Web-based tools and practices in higher education at that time. Because the world of cyberspace is evolving rapidly—"virtual" generations are measured in months, not years—examples, Web links, and even institutions discussed in the paper may be quickly out-of-date or extinct. The central ideas and issues, however, should have a much longer life, hopefully framing discussions until the Millennium and beyond.

Decisionmakers who are concerned with these technical and policy issues are a main audience for this report. It should also be of interest to academic, research, and business professionals who are concerned with applications of information technology in education and the social implications of those applications.

The study was sponsored by the California Education Round Table. It was carried out under the auspices of RAND Education, directed by Dr. Roger Benjamin.

For further information on this study, contact

Roger Benjamin (Roger_Benjamin@rand.org),
Matthew Lewis (Matthew_Lewis@rand.org), or
David McArthur (David_McArthur@rand.org).

This report is also accessible on the World Wide Web at

http://www.rand.org/publications/MR/MR975/

In the online version, the Web sites mentioned here are represented by active links to the sites themselves.

CONTENTS

FIGURES

SUMMARY

Until very recently, discussions of the crisis in U.S. education centered exclusively on public schools in the United States; higher education has been viewed as almost trouble-free—the best in the world. Today, however, several problems loom. Many states' budgets for higher education are falling, and some are poised for truly terrifying reductions even as student populations are increasing and becoming more diverse (in age as well as ethnic composition). At the same time, even as resources are shrinking, industries and consumers are demanding more of colleges. Further, a broad shift from manual workers to "knowledge workers" means that students will require more education; high school diplomas no longer guarantee good job prospects. And many predict that job skills will need updating every few years; if so, "lifelong learners" will continue to demand education and retraining throughout their careers. All these changes are straining institutions of higher education to the breaking point.

In this report, we look broadly at the prospects of meeting some of these challenges with a new generation of information technologies. We review and analyze, in particular, the emerging global information infrastructure—the first pieces of which we now see in the Internet and World Wide Web—and the multiple roles they can play in higher education:

- to improve learning and teaching
- to improve the creation of instruction and learning materials
- to create educational communities

- to compete with new providers
- to address policy and planning issues.

IMPROVING LEARNING AND TEACHING

As resources for higher education dwindle, many now look to information technologies to improve productivity by reducing the time, money, and teaching resources needed to help students learn. In the past, distance-learning applications have demonstrated some of the most impressive cost savings. Several lines of evidence suggest that the Web may be the most cost-effective way to deliver distance-learning courses in the future. Classes from the World Lecture Hall Web site, for example, already incorporate a wealth of multimedia material, including lecture overheads and annotations, digitized lecture audio, digital archives of past final exams, pointers to online libraries, and even interactive simulations that can be run at a distance. To support multi-person, multimedia dialogues in real-time, high-bandwidth interactivity will be available soon. The new generation of Internet-based distance-learning courses, therefore, should provide substantially richer learning experiences for students than the current generation does. At the broadest level, an Internet style of learning or instruction delivery will be so common that distance learning will no longer be viewed as a special form of education delivery.

Many applications of information technology in education are aimed at reducing costs. Since Internet and Web tools will continue to drop in cost and increase in functionality for the foreseeable future, information technology should continue to displace more and more faculty labor. Further, what labor cannot be displaced will at least not have to be nearby; the Internet can connect students with faculty and peers as easily as it connects learners with multimedia documents. Eventually, then, most learning will be distance-independent, and the special cases will be those that are geographically bound.

Other applications focus on the "output" side of the productivity equation: helping students learn more or better, or to learn new skills—skills rarely included in higher-education curricula. For example, intelligent tutoring systems, which try to capture in software much of the reasoning and knowledge of expert tutors, have led to some dramatic improvements in student learning (e.g., SHERLOCK provides four years of on-the-job training in 20 to 30 hours). More-innovative applications of information technology follow a very different principle: Instead of mimicking human tutors, they provide rich, simulated environments that enable students or trainees to practice skills intensively. Although today many of these applications run only on high-powered machines, emerging standards will soon permit them to be accessed by students who might have only low-end machines—and almost any kind of low-end machine, not just those the original application developer envisioned.

While many applications clearly intend to help speed up learning or improve learning of well-defined subject areas, it is much less obvious how others improve educational productivity in any simple sense. Information technology is also a driver of educational reform, not of productivity enhancement—unless "productivity" is redefined to include a wide range of qualitative changes, not just quantitative improvements. Such applications are trying to transform the *processes* and *products* of learning. For example, they might exploit new visualization technologies to enable junior students to learn about complex systems that previously only graduate students found comprehensible; or they could foster deeper understanding through inquiry-based learning rather than traditional lectures, or through collaborative learning methods that never existed before high-bandwidth networks.

IMPROVING THE CREATION OF INSTRUCTION AND LEARNING MATERIALS

In addition to providing tools for teachers and learners, information technology can help create new instruction and learning material, improve its organization, facilitate access to it, and speed its development. Many parts make up the traditional pipeline for producing educational materials (and intellectual artifacts, in general), but four are central: authors create documents; publishers mainly manufacture and market copies of these products; libraries primarily acquire, store, and distribute copies to the nearby community; and readers consume them. These groups have played relatively stable roles in the publication process for decades, even centuries. However, information technology is changing their roles; and, equally important, it is transforming the copyright and intellectual-property-rights laws that underpin relationships among the groups.

In the simplest view of this change, new information technologies will appear to reduce, perhaps even eliminate, the need for publishers and libraries. Traditional academic publishers have approached the Internet very reluctantly, because the Web calls up their worst nightmare: They sell one copy of a digital book, then all others are produced for free with a few mouse clicks. Compared with larger traditional publishing firms, small, grassroots publishers on the Web appear to be more flexible providers of new digital courseware, helping higher education to meet the rising need for "just-in-time" or "on-demand" learning just as information technology already helps manufacturing and services industries dramatically shorten production cycles.

Providing a location and supporting tools that encourage faculty not only to create new online course materials but to share them with others, Web sites such as the World Lecture Hall already demonstrate some of this flexibility. Because the Hall is implemented as a Web homepage, all materials from a course can be downloaded, with minimal effort, from the Hall site to the browser's home machine. This copy can be edited into a new course, possibly one for a slightly different topic and audience, using simple digital cut-and-paste tools. The new version can be returned to the World Lecture Hall, adding again to the materials available to be shared with the academic community. Eventually, this kind of "chaotic cooperation" might lead to a vast collection of digital courses of progressively better and better quality, as a new generation of course creators stands on the shoulders of the current creators.

This kind of highly informal cross-institutional collaboration has been common in academic research. But, in the past, most higher-education institutions have been much more reluctant to share their course offerings, informally or otherwise. Individual academic publishing, therefore, may stress or even transform existing institutional structures, rather than simply enabling them to operate more productively without fundamental change.

CREATING EDUCATIONAL COMMUNITIES

The World Lecture Hall is one of many new academic and learning communities that are beginning to flourish across the Web. Organized along functional lines, most of these communities are developing courseware, conducting research, and sharing curricula, among other things. Common interests and expertise are much more important in defining these communities than is distance, which is largely erased by cheap, high-bandwidth connectivity. For similar reasons, most cyberspace communities tend to ignore institutional boundaries when those boundaries interfere with emerging functional interests. These factors are beginning to give rise to new communities of practice that, at the very least, crisscross previous structures and, in the extreme, can erode old higher-education structures while building new ones.

Virtual universities, a few of which already exist as prototypes, may be the most extensive (and certainly most publicized) examples of electronic communities. Not extensions of existing institutions, some of the most comprehensive virtual universities on the Internet have been created in cyberspace almost from scratch. Although they by no means rival their traditional counterparts in faculty size or range of courses, online universities such as Athena are beginning to put together digital versions of all the familiar pieces of a campus. Like a typical university, Athena grants liberal arts degrees, has a transfer-credit policy, and offers a detailed and surprisingly traditional core curriculum—quite consciously an attempt to capture in a virtual version the best of traditional university structure. Athena differs substantially from most higher-education institutions only in its admission policy (because finite resources such as classroom space are not an issue, enrollment is open and unlimited) and its teaching methods.

Unlike Athena, a few groups are viewing cyberspace as an opportunity to rethink the structure of educational institutions from the foundations up, rather than as a new tool for an existing organization. The Globewide Network Academy (GNA), one such experiment, is, in a broad sense, a mix of Athena and the World Lecture Hall. Like Athena (and unlike the World Lecture Hall), GNA offers more than just a collection of online courses; it also includes virtual discussion lounges, where teachers, students, administrative and support staff, and technical experts can engage in ongoing electronic discussions about the academy. The student lounge also contains a collection of links that constitute an ad hoc digital library, and another set of links to career resources. Like the World Lecture Hall (and unlike Athena), however, GNA is not developing its own courses. Rather, it encourages institutions and individuals to list with GNA existing courses for online distance learning, and then provides a collection of value-added and brokering services to help students find the courseware they want and to put them in contact with the providing institutions. At the same time, GNA offers support services for teachers and contributing institutions, which are expected to improve the quantity and quality of the products GNA manages.

In general, higher-education institutions have been reluctant to experiment with more novel designs of a GNA for using information technology: Not only are newer ideas tougher to devise and more expensive to implement, but digitizing old institutions may still seem like a perfectly serviceable, and much more certain, strategy. However, if current higher-education institutions are not interested in conducting high-risk experiments, new external providers of educational services are more than willing to try. If they succeed, they may make clinging to the status quo less and less tenable.

COMPETING WITH NEW PROVIDERS

For decades, providers of education external to traditional colleges and universities have offered a variety of courses and services—from full degrees to short courses and training seminars. Of this sector, the biggest (over $50 billion per year) and certainly fastest-growing (more than 15 percent per year) part belongs to companies that provide corporate training—everything from mastering the nuances of Windows 95 to acquiring much more generic skills in object-oriented programming, analysis, and design. Such courses generally come from external providers specializing in training products that make the heaviest, and often most innovative, uses of information technology.

Higher education's challenges in competing with these new external providers are, if anything, exacerbated by information technology, not eased. Information technology has helped proprietary providers reduce delivery costs to the point where even "down-market" (read: higher-education) services can be delivered profitably. Unfortunately, higher-education institutions, as a whole, have not formulated plans to deal with the increasing encroachment of external providers on their turf. They need to.

Several options—only a few of which have been tried seriously—are worth considering. One approach is to shore up defenses against invaders into traditional higher-education markets by erecting protectionist barriers (such as tax supports) that discourage new providers from entering the battle. Perhaps a more positive tactic is to improve productivity in the face of new competition. Many of the enterprises we reviewed—distance-learning campuses and virtual universities, for example—can be regarded as ways in which higher education is already trying to become more productive, sometimes by borrowing models of delivery from the training sector and often by creating innovative models of its own.

A different strategy—to take the offensive rather than honing defenses—is inspired in part by movements of external providers into higher education's turf. A few institutions are beginning to respond to the challenges posed by external providers by moving, however cautiously, into contract training. This strategy is difficult, however, not only because external providers have a wealth of experience, cash, and technology, but because existing institutional policies often handicap higher education from the outset. For example, whereas business clients frequently expect to be able to mix their instructors with college personnel, college union contracts may forbid hiring external staff.

ADDRESSING POLICY ISSUES AND PLANNING

The preceding discussion raises a number of research questions and policy issues about whether applications of the Internet and Web in higher education are technically and economically feasible—and, if so, how institutions should design their technology plans to make best use of these technologies. We focus here on just a few key questions and policy recommendations.

How Will Higher Education Acquire Sufficient Internet Infrastructure?

Technical feasibility poses perhaps the greatest barrier to moving higher education onto the Internet and Web comprehensively. Many higher-education institutions are now developing and implementing technology plans for distance learning around technologies with much less functionality than the Web will shortly offer—for example, videotape sent through the mail, one-way TV (over cable channels) augmented with two-way audio (through telephones), or two-way video conferencing using special-purpose hardware. To some of them, a proposal to use the Internet and Web for fully interactive, high-bandwidth, and multimedia courseware must look very premature.

We argue that such a proposal is not premature. Further, we suggest that commercialization, sometimes viewed as a threat to the small academic community that used to be cyberspace, is instead a key to making the necessary broadband infrastructure available both widely and cheaply. To realize this opportunity, however, higher education should take the following steps—and quickly, since windows of opportunity are beginning to close:

- *Coordinate technology plans and purchases.* The simplest step that higher-education institutions—actually, *all* educational institutions—should take is to change their model for technology acquisition. Today, schools at all levels buy, piecemeal, hardware, infrastructure, software, and support services for computers and networking. When buying stand-alone computers, this practice is merely unfortunate: Bulk purchases are much cheaper. But when acquiring networking infrastructure, it is a catastrophic error: Networks that cannot interoperate are nearly useless.
- *Exploit the Telecommunications Act of 1996.* State and federal debates are now setting the stage for regulations that will influence the quantity, quality, distribution, and cost of telecommunication infrastructure and services over the coming decades. This act, signed into law by President Clinton in February 1996, touches on a wide range of issues that pertain to communications giants, electronic publishers, the entertainment media, and

educators. With the act's passage, many think the best window of opportunity to influence policy in ways that will benefit education is now closed. In fact, the act ignores several critical issues, delegates some decisions, and defers others to later dates. Internet capabilities available to higher education, and their costs, may depend on the outcome of political debates still to come in Washington and the states. To influence these debates, institutions of higher education should unite behind a broad, common vision of their goals and the technology required to achieve those goals.

- *Pursue options for inexpensive end-user machines.* Even if higher-education institutions can secure the infrastructure needed to supply generous amounts of richly interactive courseware across the Internet, students will still need to interact comfortably and cheaply with these products. Many already can, of course. But if education on the Internet is to be as readily available as education in the classroom, students of all ages will need almost universal access to online courseware. Today, this is not the case, although several options are emerging that might meet this need: Internet appliances may drop in price to a point where most students can afford them, universities could supply machines for students (some already do), libraries and other community services could provide Internet access, manufacturers might consider pay terminals (analogous to pay telephones), and governments could use vouchers as well as other forms of cross-subsidy. The costs and policy implications of these and other potential solutions must be analyzed carefully.

How Will Higher Education Acquire Quality Courseware and Educate Staff?

Universities and students who enjoy lavish Internet capacity will still need quality Web products for learning that make good use of this capacity; in turn, faculty will need to acquire the tools and skills with which to create Web-based distance-learning courseware. Many have argued that the cost of developing new products and providing faculty education will be prohibitive, especially in view of shrinking budgets in higher education. To the contrary, we suggest that much of the necessary training can be accomplished within existing budgets, provided colleges and universities are willing to adopt some of the following creative solutions.

- *Use existing tools and training.* Many of the tools needed to develop Web-based courseware, and most of the training needed to become proficient with these tools, are already available. We recommend that universities adopt them rather than developing their own. Certainly, higher education will need to revamp many programs to help faculty acquire new teaching skills that are better suited to technology-intensive classrooms, which, in the future, will be less dominated by lecture and more driven by collaborative projects or online mentoring. But to delegate all training on Web publishing to schools of education might risk duplicating many services already offered by online communities—yet another case of new electronic communities that crisscross the boundaries of traditional higher-education institutions. Higher education must find strategies for coordinating with electronic communities, if only because much of the literature and training they offer is good, and free.
- *Shift staff time from teaching to creating courseware.* Courses and communities might help faculty acquire skills in Web-based courseware development, but one big question remains: Where will the money come from to pay for the acquisition, to say nothing of the time? We suggest that it can be done at roughly current levels of funding, provided faculty can reallocate the time they devote to their various teaching activities. Since information technology is slowly beginning to displace faculty by performing some of their traditional teaching roles, staff could spend more time creating courseware. If the transition from lecture-intensive curricula to Web-based courseware is managed reasonably, the added course-development time may come at little or no increased cost to higher-education institutions.
- *Nourish grassroots publication.* Higher-education institutions can also encourage the development of quality Web courseware through tactics that help foster and manage the grassroots, or individual, publishing that we see taking shape in online communities such as the World Lecture Hall. Universities and colleges could follow GNA's lead, for example, and provide a common infrastructure for online courses. Perhaps they would do

even better to copy proprietary institutions (such as Microsoft's OnLine Institute), which supply value-added services that establish goals and areas for new courseware, offer technical assistance to courseware developers, and furnish quality-control standards. In addition, setting standards for courseware format (to ensure interoperability) will probably be as important as establishing content standards. Overall, the intent of these tactics must be to foster a culture of sharing in online communities of higher education.

How Will Higher Education Choose Among Many Models for Using the Internet and Web?

Assuming higher education has the financial, physical, and human resources necessary to use the Web and Internet, what structures or models should it adopt to deliver educational services? Perhaps both the biggest blessing and biggest challenge of the Internet is that it makes possible so many alternative models for learning, teaching, and education delivery. We cannot recommend a single model. Rather, we suggest that higher-education institutions examine many possible models, choosing and tailoring those that are most consistent with their missions and financial constraints, and that also take into account the imminent sea changes in the educational market: the growth of new private providers, the increasing diversity of student populations, and the rapid turnover of skills in emerging knowledge-based industries.

We further recommend that higher-education institutions deliberately attempt to consider models that call into question as many features of traditional institutions as possible—for instance, the length of courses, the size of classes, the bundling of now-separable services such as courseware creation, delivery, and student credentialing. Specific questions might include:

- Is it reasonable to consider creating ultra-short courses that can be aggregated by students into highly tailored educational experiences, on an as-needed basis?
- To what extent, and under what conditions is it possible to develop technology-intensive distance-learning courses that offer

open (or at least dramatically increased) student enrollment, while keeping course quality high?

- Should all institutions be developers of educational courseware, or is there a role for value-added course brokers and repackagers?
- More generally, to what extent is it now technically feasible, and economically sensible to unbundle the value-chain of educational services traditionally offered by higher-education institutions—ranging from course-content creation, to reselling, to marketing, to brokering, to distribution?

We recommend these "what if" experiments not necessarily because traditional institutional structures are terribly flawed, but because alternatives resembling familiar models are likely to be explored while less-familiar ones go unnoticed. More than anything else, we hope to initiate discussion of these unusual, and sometimes useful, alternatives.

CONCLUSION

Our analysis suggests many reasons for optimism. However, we do not regard information technologies as an unqualified answer to the problems of higher education. Many of the most effective uses of technologies will not improve productivity in higher education in any simple sense; rather, they will transform the processes and products of learning and teaching. As a result, they may threaten the current structure of the university more than just streamline it. Such transformations will have costs as well as benefits, and the prospect of fundamental structural change will require that policy issues be addressed not only by higher-education institutions but by state and federal governments.

Chapter One

INTRODUCTION AND OVERVIEW

Until very recently, discussions of the crisis in U.S. education centered exclusively on public schools in the United States; higher education has been viewed as almost trouble-free—the best in the world. Today, however, several problems loom. Many states' budgets for higher education are falling, and some are poised for truly terrifying reductions even as student populations are increasing and becoming more diverse (in age as well as ethnic composition). At the same time, even as resources are shrinking, industries and consumers are demanding more of colleges. Further, a broad shift from manual workers to "knowledge workers" means that students will require more education; high school diplomas no longer guarantee good job prospects. And many predict that job skills will need updating every few years; if so, "lifelong learners" will continue to demand education and retraining throughout their careers. All these changes are straining institutions of higher education to the breaking point.

Information technologies have played a vital role in higher education for decades. Television started sending instruction to campuses and homes during the 1950s (remember Sunrise Semester?); before that, radio and film were used in a wide range of courses; and computers have populated labs in schools since the late 1960s. But only recently has interest in educational applications of information technology, which now includes the Internet and the World Wide Web, reached nearly universal proportions. In the past, discussion of educational technology was limited mainly to academic and teaching journals; now, almost every major newspaper has devoted at least a series of articles or a Sunday supplement to "Learning in Cyberspace," touting technology as a savior for education.

As veterans in the battle to move computers into classrooms, we in the Institute on Education and Training at RAND are naturally excited by this surge of interest. But we are also anxious, because this is not the first time technology has been touted as a savior for education, and all previous technology "revolutions" have failed, in part because they were not, technically, great improvements on prior educational tools. Of course, past failures have not been complete flops; after all, the use of instructional TV and computer-based integrated learning systems, for example, persists in schools and campuses, although mainly on the margin. And newer technologies, from CD-ROM-based multimedia products to Internet chat rooms, are potentially much more powerful than previous technologies; so they should avoid many prior technical limitations. However, like the previous technology revolutions, the impending information-technology revolution also may fall far short of expectations.

With the hope that we can help the revolution move forward, we offer here a critical, constructive review of the potential opportunities that new information technologies afford higher education.

A QUALIFIED VISION

We admit, at the outset, that we believe that information technologies can help higher education reach many of its goals. We will go even further to say that our vision is organized around the *pervasive use of interactive and high-bandwidth communication networks.* In particular, the model we champion is the Internet, the World Wide Web (WWW), and its generic tools (e.g., browsers such as Netscape), which are used to create and run applications (now often called "homepages"). But it is not the early Web (as late as 1995), with its static book pages rendered electronically, that we think could revolutionize education and learning. It is, instead, the emerging global information infrastructure (GII) of dynamic Web objects that will succeed the current Internet and WWW—a computational environment populated by many multimedia and interactive applications, as well as human and computer agents—which will be the focus of our discussions.

Higher-education institutions, in general, are very well represented on the Internet. This is hardly surprising: For its first 25 years, the Internet (until 1990 called the ARPANET) was inhabited mainly by universities, nonprofits, and government agencies. True, some colleges and smaller universities still lag behind, but the larger schools remain among the most extensive and most sophisticated users of Internet and Web resources—even today, as commercial sites rapidly take over cyberspace. Put most positively, the Internet is probably the only information-technology arena in which higher education has more than kept pace with the business world, both in its raw capacity and its skill in creating useful products. (On a given day, the average university classroom surely logs more Web-site "hits" than phone calls.)

Of course, many technologies other than the Internet can and do play important roles in education. Stand-alone computers run many kinds of useful instructional programs; they will continue to be important as machines drop in price even as they increase in power. And, today certainly, more educational information is delivered on CD-ROM than through networks such as the Internet. Still, we favor the Internet as a unique foundation for education because it will *eventually* include all the functionalities of the other available tools, and more. Rooted in relatively primitive network applications that transfer files of text (e.g., ftp), over the past few years, the World Wide Web has added layer upon layer of new communication protocols and document types. Now you can find Web sites that imitate almost all other communication devices and genres—audio or video, two-way or one-way, broadcast or point-to-point. But are these imitations? Perhaps it is better to view the Internet simply as a flexible new medium that can merge or encompass all old (and new) information technologies. A few of the Web sites that are chameleons masquerading as other media are summarized in Figure 1.1. (This list was compiled in May 1997.) While the Internet can mimic more-traditional information media and genres, it also offers novel functionalities not found elsewhere—multi-user video games (such as "Quake"; http://www.idsoftware.com/), interactive soap operas (such as "The Spot"; http://www.thespot.com/),[1] and online "chat" rooms (such as "V-Chat"; http://www.microsoft.com/ie/chat/), for instance.

[1]Some of the Web site URLs given in this document are broken at the ends of text lines, for typographical purposes. However, they should be read as unbroken character strings with no intercharacter spaces.

Function	*Web Site Example*
Radio	***NPR's*** site (http://www.npr.org/) includes many of their programs, current and past, including newscasts updated every hour. ***Net Radio*** (http://www.netradio.net/) permits listeners to select different types of music, as well as "talk radio" features, at a click of the mouse. Both NPR and Net Radio use ***Real Audio*** (http://www.realaudio.com/) as a helper application.
Telephone	VocalTec's ***Internet Phone*** (http://www.vocaltec.com/) provides telephone-quality, point-to-point, voice communication over the Internet. Internet Phone incurs no long-distance charges, much to the consternation of traditional long-distance providers.
Television	Many Web sites are already devoted to commercial TV; most are simply advertising, but several include substantial video. ***PBS***'s "Life on the Internet" (http://www.pbs.org/internet/) was a 13-part video series made available on the Internet. It used ***VDOLive's*** (http://www.vdolive.com/) Internet video technology and servers. ***HyperTV*** (http://www.hypertv.com/) promises to interweave traditional TV transmission and Internet browsing. ***MSN*** (http://www.msn.com/) acts more like a TV network than a single TV channel or program.
Newspaper	Hundreds of newspapers are now online. Some are faithful to their hardcopy versions; others are better designed for the Web. In this regard, ***The New York Times on the Web*** (http://www.nytimes.com/) falls about in the middle.
Phone book	***BigBook*** (http://www.bigbook.com/) not only boasts a very complete interactive Yellow Pages for the whole nation, but also will display a map showing the location of a business, as well as reviews offered by other users.
Billboard	***CyberBillboard*** (http://village.ios.com/~cyber/cbbdesgn.htm) will design and post digital billboards on the Web for customers.
Fax	There are any number of ways to send a fax on the Internet. Try just printing, say, a Word document to a fax "printer."
CD-ROM-based video game	As the Internet's multimedia capacity has expanded, ***Nintendo*** (http://www.nintendo.com/), ***Sega*** (http://www.sega.com/), and other video game companies that used to distribute products either on CD-ROMs or cartridges have made many new and old titles available on the Web.
Intelligent tutoring systems	***Rebel!*** is an interactive, exploratory environment for learning history through simulation. It was originally configured as a standalone application, running on a Macintosh; but it was reconfigured to display to, and interact with, users on any machine connected to the Web.

Figure 1.1—The Internet and World Wide Web As Communication Chameleons

Supported by emerging standards such as the Common Object Request Broker Architecture (CORBA), new document formats (now called distributed objects) and communication protocols will evolve into an ever-expanding collection. These will give rise to more and more genres unique to digital networks—products that imitate no previous forms of communication.

If interaction is omitted, the Internet can become instructional TV; if text and other symbolic media are omitted, it can mimic two-way video; if multi-casting is omitted, the Internet might look like a one-on-one intelligent tutoring system; the Internet can even impersonate fax, radio, and newspapers. The ability of the emerging Internet to encompass just about all other information technologies is potentially critical to realizing its value for higher education.

Qualifications on the Vision: Why the Road to Revolution Might Be Rocky

In addition to discussing how this potential could be realized in higher education, we insert a recurring theme that provides a sober counterpoint to this promising picture. We claim that information technology—or any profound innovation—leads to a fairly predictable sequence of events as it is adopted in society:

- First, it is exploited as an *enhancer*, or magnifier. The innovation is used to accomplish traditional practices (in manufacturing, services industries, even education) more efficiently or productively.
- Later, it becomes a *transformer*. It leads to new practices and products, not simply better versions of traditional ones. This shift is usually very slow and rarely smooth.

Traditional applications of new technologies can lead to improvements that are more valuable than the original version of the technology, so there is often good reason to resist fundamental change. For example, early gas-powered vehicles designed to resemble horseless carriages *are* useful. But, in the long run, the technology affords new opportunities that can be more valuable: Cars are *much more* useful. Yet this transformation is not without great uncertainty and great cost—in time, money, and fundamental restructuring.

Cars dominate carriages only if we build paved roads, provide service stations, and pass laws that govern speed and the transport of goods.

This idea is not new (it parallels the economic distinction between *process* and *product innovation,* for example) but will arise often in our discussions. We discuss many possible applications of information technologies in higher education. Some relatively traditional applications are attractive in the short term because they can help cut costs. There is certainly no reason to reject them. But innovative applications could help solve other important problems in the long term, even though they may not save money in the short term. The difficulty is that some of these applications are not just technology fixes or add-ons; they will require that the higher-education community think hard about its mission, its organization, and its willingness to invest in change—even in a time of fiscal tightening.

THE PLAN

Our discussion begins with examples that illustrate many interesting, cutting-edge applications. But, unlike many discussions of education in cyberspace, our focus is on information technology as a tool to help solve the central problems in higher education. We consider:

- the need to reduce costs and to increase productivity in the face of dwindling resources
- the challenges of an expanding and increasingly diverse student population (including minorities and geographically isolated rural or inner-city populations, as well as lifelong learners who must retool their skills)
- the necessity of adapting to changes in industry and social demands (a broad shift away from manual laborers and toward knowledge workers)
- competition with a growing number of external providers—proprietary, for-profit firms not associated with colleges or universities (often specializing in corporate training but almost always exploiting information technology).

Information technologies can affect many facets of higher education, much as they do almost every service industry. We focus here on the opportunities that appear unique to education, ignoring many important applications. For example, we pass over the different ways technologies already streamline student-record maintenance, budgeting, payroll, and general administration. There is already a large body of literature on the costs and benefits to business of computer and communication technologies, and educational applications add few new insights to this field. Rather, we look at applications of information technologies from the inner missions of higher education outward:

- the benefits for learning and instruction delivery that new information technologies can promise
- the ways in which information technologies can help provide tools for building instruction
- the tools information technologies can offer for improving decisionmaking and community-building within higher education
- the manner in which information technologies can help connect higher-education institutions to industry and society as a whole.

In these discussions we summarize available data on how technology helps overcome important challenges to higher education. But we also include many sidebars of current or emerging "best practice." Our arguments are illustrated by anecdotes, or examples, partly because they bring abstract claims to life and partly because there are few hard data on what new technologies can really do for higher education.

We next summarize the evidence about these applications to clarify those that are less than they seem; uncover others that may be more promising, although perhaps less obviously so or less colorful; and identify the hidden costs—costs that must be paid if even the most promising uses of information technology in higher education are to deliver what they suggest. This summary leads to a more complete discussion of the barriers to realizing the potentials of new technologies in higher education and, finally, to some broad policy issues that surround the resolution of these problems.

Chapter Two

BENEFITS FOR LEARNING AND INSTRUCTION DELIVERY

Information technologies might improve learning and teaching in two distinct ways. Just as they have made workers more productive in business and commerce, they could reduce teaching costs or increase the speed with which learners acquire knowledge. Alternatively, such technologies might help improve the quality of learning, rather than simply making it faster and cheaper. In this section we first review evidence that information technologies can improve the efficiency of learning and teaching; then we consider how they might lead to better educational outcomes.

REDUCING COSTS AND INCREASING PRODUCTIVITY

Most discussions of computers in education look at how new technologies might improve "instruction delivery," a management theorist's way of saying how teachers teach and how learners learn. Therefore, as resources for higher education continue to dwindle, when most people think of information technologies, it will usually be in terms of how such technologies might reduce the number of teachers needed or cut the time (and money) it takes learners to acquire skills. A collection of cases in current practice suggests that some technologies do indeed help improve productivity in these ways. (See Figure 2.1.)

Current successes are subject to several qualifications. Some cost savings are modest, others come with hidden prices (for example, high development costs or lower graduation rates), and all depend on careful attention to implementation in the classroom. But, although the data are still unclear, the economic logic behind the view is relatively straightforward: Cut costs by doing more with less; that is, hold student outcomes roughly constant (or improving) while displacing labor (staff) with capital (here, information technology). With technology costs continually dropping while labor costs only rise, this trade-off appears a good one for increasing productivity.

Site/Study	*Cost-effectiveness Results*
Computer-Aided Instruction (CAI)) and Computer-Based Instruction (CBT)	
Orlansky and String (1979)	-30 percent reduction in time to achieve criterion performance using computer-based instruction in military training
Fletcher (summary of 47 studies) (1991)	-30 percent time savings, 30-40 percent cost savings, and improved achievement using multimedia instruction
Levin (summary of 8 programs) (1989)	-CAI proved more cost-effective than reducing class size or extending length of school day -but less effective than peer tutoring
Hall (summary of 8 case studies) 1995	-CBT in business reduced training time 40 to 80 percent compared with traditional text-based training -CBT in business reduced training costs 40 to 85 percent compared with traditional training
Roberts (1991)	-IBM cut its annual training budget (over $1 billion) by $30 million by using CBT
Intelligent Tutoring Systems (ITS)	
U.S Air Force	-ITS traditionally deliver high student learning outcomes, but at a high price; the Air Force aims to cut development costs by 95 percent and development time by up to 80 percent -the result would be an overall reduction in training costs

Figure 2.1—Information Technology and Cost Savings
(continued on next page)

Distance Learning	
Open University, United Kingdom (1989)	-cost per graduate lower than conventional university's
Deakin University, Australia (1989)	-cost per student 97 percent that of on-campus student
Indira Gandhi National Open University, India (1991)	-cost per student between 8 and 40 percent of cost at conventional university
	-student performance rates only 60 percent
Open University teacher training, Indonesia (1988)	-cost per student about 60 percent of cost at conventional university
Everyman University, Israel (1978)	-cost per graduate estimated at one-half cost at conventional university
Teacher training at a distance, Tanzania (1979/1984)	-costs about one-half those at a conventional university
National Technological University, USA (1989)	-break-even point (in per-student cost) at 9,000 students in 200 courses

SOURCES: Distance-learning results summarized from Perraton (1994, p. 21); CAI and CBT results summarized from http://www.whitehouse.gov/WH/New/edtech/perform.html, except for Hall and Roberts results, which are summarized from Hall (1995).

Figure 2.1—(continued)

CAI and CBT

Computer-aided instruction (CAI) and computer-based training (CBT) have shown some ability to do more with less, by providing learners drill-and-practice systems that replace teachers in routine coaching tasks. These systems are most frequently found in secondary schools but also play a role in remedial math, science, and language courses at the collegiate level, as well as in business and military training (Figure 2.1). However, as convenient as they might be for self-paced learning, CBT programs often do not yield dramatic cost savings. Development costs for multimedia courseware are usually very high, often offsetting savings in delivery, and the price of a stand-alone computer system for each student is sometimes so dear that labor costs must fall dramatically before any net savings appears. The latter situation may change in the future, however, as powerful machines drop roughly to the cost of a top-of-the-line TV.

Distance Learning

A few intelligent tutoring systems (ITS) also have reported cost-reductions in training. (See Figure 2.2.) But, as with CAI and CBT, development costs currently impose strong limits on their productivity gains. In fact, the main attraction of ITS is that they may improve the quality of learning rather than reduce costs, as we discuss later under "Increasing Quality and Productivity."

Today, distance learning—whereby students and teachers rely on electronic and hardcopy media, rather than on face-to-face contact, for at least some of their communication (correspondence courses by postal mail are perhaps the oldest form of distance learning)—provides probably the best examples of cost savings that are at least partly attributable to information technologies. In this country, the PLATO system,[1] among others, pioneered distance learning in the 1960s, connecting as many as one thousand student-terminals at a time to mainframes. Only relatively recently, however, have these trailblazing ideas translated into reduced education costs. Several studies (Figure 2.1) show that distance-learning courses in Asia cost from 45 to 90 percent of the cost of conventional college classes, with comparable student performance; costs can drop to as little as 8 percent of on-campus courses, although completion rates then also seem to dip. Using telecommunications to offer distance learning for over three decades, the Open University in Great Britain—one of the first very large-scale experiments in distance learning at the higher-education level—boasts average per-student costs of around one-half those of conventional campuses. (See Figure 2.2.) We briefly examine its success to show why, at least right now, distance learning can help reduce costs only under relatively narrow circumstances.

The Open University: An Example in Achieving Cost Reductions. First, the technology must allow many students to be taught at once. Class sizes at the Open University usually exceed 200. The larger the

---

[1]For all its illustrious history, good discussions of the PLATO system are rare. One brief but broad history can be found at http://www.tencore.com/plato.htm.

> The best-known example in higher education, and most successful example of its kind in the world, is the UK Open University. Some 40 distance teaching institutions across the world have been based on the OU model. It's methods are well known, but it is worth emphasizing an important aspect that is often misunderstood. Although the OU has developed widely admired methods for the use of teams in the design and production of teaching resources, mainly paper-based materials, and although it still carries in many people's minds the image of the "University of the Air," it is the UK-wide network of part-time tutors who provide the main teaching that is experienced by OU students. Tutorial support is provided by traveling to quite frequent face-to-face meetings, by telephone contact, and by feedback on written assignments. In a real sense, the formal aspects of studying for an OU degree differ little from those experienced by students on a conventional campus. The cost per student, however, is about one-half that of conventional campus universities. The OU is now exploring how best to build on its success through the emerging advanced learning technology (ALT), in particular the use of CMC (computer-mediated communication) for collaborative learning and the delivery of its course materials through CD-ROM (from Mayes, 1994; http://www.icbl.hw.ac.uk/ctl/mayes/ paper10.html).

Figure 2.2—The Open University: Mother of Modern Distance Learning

class size, the greater the student–teacher ratio, which lowers labor costs and spreads high development and initial technology costs, leading, in turn, to productivity improvements. Break-even points—class sizes for which the cost of distance education and traditional delivery are roughly equal—will vary depending on, among other things, the size of technology investment and the course being taught. But it is a safe bet, at least for the near term, that distance-learning classes of less than 20 will rarely lead to substantial per-student cost reductions.

Second, a substantial amount of labor must be displaced by technology. Typically, labor is over 95 percent the cost of the class; so, modest trades of faculty for machines will not substantially change overall prices. Consequently, distance learning works best in relatively "standard" courses—math and the sciences—for which knowledge is relatively routine, can be embedded in the technology, and can have much teaching delegated to it. Alternatively, to expand the range of courses that can be taught at a distance, the use of technology should be carefully designed so that expensive labor at least can be replaced by cheaper help. For example, the Open University makes liberal use of tutors (replacing many full professors), either in person or on the phone.

Third, technology should substitute for labor as simply as possible. As the example of the Open University suggests, most low-cost distance learning does not fundamentally change the learning experience for the student, or the teacher. A computer application that promised to play a substantial role in teaching but that also demanded broad changes in faculty skills and activities (several of which are discussed in Chapters Three and Four) could actually increase labor costs, even while guaranteeing a savings in teacher time.

The bottom line, then, is that today's distance-learning technology is largely limited to imparting relatively routine skills and knowledge, taught *en masse,* through relatively traditional methods. Most of the best examples actually come from military and corporate training, rather than from higher education. For example, large companies such as Ford now contract for distance instruction to help their employees learn how to use tools such as spreadsheets and word processors, as well as specialized equipment. And Hewlett-Packard estimates that it saves millions of dollars each year using distance learning to train employees more effectively and more efficiently than with conventional methods. These examples explain why well over one-half of distance learning now goes on not in academic settings but in businesses—a market that is expanding so rapidly that whole TV networks are now dedicated to corporate distance learning.

The Internet is increasingly being viewed as a medium that can bring distance learning and its cost benefits into the higher-education sector. In the next subsection, we look at the cost and other advantages the Internet in particular can provide as a distance-learning tool for higher-education institutions.

Internet Impact: Distance Learning, Cost Reduction, and Increased Access

At least partly to cut costs, almost all higher-education institutions in the United States are considering distance-learning programs, dozens already have substantial offerings in place, and many universities are now moving in this direction. In the future, we believe that the Internet will be the most cost-effective way to deliver a new generation of distance-learning courses. By winter 1996, the U.S. Distance Learning Association (http://www.usdla.org/home.html) listed many dozens of universities with homepages outlining their WWW and Internet-based courseware. At the same time, the World Lecture Hall, a Web site managed by the University of Texas, has become a "virtual repository," organizing links to hundreds of other sites that are making Web-based class materials available to anyone who is interested. (See Chapter Three for a more complete description of the World Lecture Hall.)

Because the WWW first came online only in 1991, all these courses are new, and there are no solid data proving the effectiveness of Internet-based distance education. But a chemistry curriculum drawn almost at random from the World Lecture Hall[2] illustrates some of the reasons why Web-based distance learning seems very promising, at least "on paper." (See Figure 2.3.) To begin with, emerging Internet courses can include a wealth of material about the class (lectures, exams, assignments) and references to relevant online literature (books, programs, tools such as the periodic table), all accessible at the click of a mouse on a hypertext link. Each of these sources can be constructed as multimedia documents, including pictures, digitized audio versions of lectures, presentation overheads—even simulations, which can be run to give a much more dynamic impression of processes and structures. Full high-bandwidth interactivity will be available soon, to support multi-person, multimedia dialogues in real-time. The new generation of

---

[2]This curriculum was found under the "Chemistry" entries on the World Lecture Hall homepage (http://www.utexas.edu/world/lecture/index.html) on February 22, 1988. The course itself was at Brown University (http://jcbmac.chem.brown.edu/baird/Chem22I/chem22i.html) on the same date.

Chemistry 22C is taught by Prof. James C. Baird of Brown University. The WWW course materials, found indexed under "Chemistry" on the World Lecture Hall, include

- online lecture notes
- lecture "overheads"
- digitized audio of actual lectures, which can be played, rewound, replayed
- homework assignments and answers, updated weekly
- electronic archives of past final exams and answers
- pointers to online resource material.

Students access these different resources just as they do any Web homepage: by pointing and clicking on text links.

While this example is quite complete, it did not include features found in a few other course homepages:

- *Calendar of class sessions.* Often presented as a table, including date of the class and daily topic. The topic description is often hypertext; clicking on it allows access to the material for the class (lectures, overheads, etc.).
- *Virtual office hours.* Some professors included buttons that allowed students to send e-mail to them or to other students in the class.
- *"Chat" rooms.* In some classes, students can login and engage in text-based discussions with other students from the class who also happen to be on at the same time. Faculty also often pre-arrange virtual office hours: times at which they will be logged-on as well.
- *Video and movie clips.* Video clips (usually less than a minute in duration, given current time and space constraints) are sometimes included in Web courseware to demonstrate complex physical processes, for example.
- *"Live" computer programs.* In an increasing number of Web-based courses, students can run simulations, in addition to viewing static lecture materials. The simulations run on remote machines, but display on the user's machine, and often permit the student to interact with the simulation and control its execution—for instance, using forms to input simulation parameters.

Figure 2.3—Internet-Based Distance Learning: Today and Tomorrow

Internet-based distance-learning courses, in short, can mix the graphics and video of instructional TV with a much more intimate style of interactive mentoring than teleconferencing ever could. Therefore, it should provide substantially richer learning experiences for students than the current generation does.

Web-based distance learning might enhance productivity in higher education in several ways. Most obviously, by providing a more powerful and flexible medium, the Web should enable developers to construct higher-quality courseware for a wider range of classes than ever before. (See Figure 2.4, top panel.) With richer courseware, classes for which computers once replaced only a modest amount of labor might shortly be taught almost exclusively through technology; and in courses in which information technology previously had no part, it may play at least a supporting role. All this means that Web-based learning tools, appropriately used, promise to replace more labor and, consequently, to lower faculty costs.

But less-visible features of Internet-based distance learning—costs and standards—may enhance productivity even more dramatically. It is reasonable to assume that if courseware built on the Web is richer than previous distance-learning products, it might also be more costly to deliver—reasonable, but probably wrong. Although few realize it, the Internet is not only a better medium for learning and interaction but a *cheaper* way to deliver instruction (Figure 2.4, bottom panel)—something providers of corporate training have already figured out. For example, corporate providers are quickly trading their old on-demand video systems for more-flexible and less-expensive high-capacity intranets, which use Internet-style communication on private networks to deliver full-motion video to hundreds of viewers at once, at the click of a mouse. (See Figure 2.5.)

Schools and homes can expect similar benefits, even if they cannot afford the high-capacity LANs of big business. High-bandwidth yet low-cost connections to the WWW will soon come in several forms. Many homes today can access the Internet cheaply through ISDN phone connections, providing about 5 to 10 times the effective bandwidth of ordinary phone lines. More interestingly, successful trials of cable modems in 1996 promise very high-speed Internet connections, at roughly the cost of standard cable service. (See

The Internet's promise for distance learning is based on its potential to provide a flexible and high-functionality medium for delivering instruction, at a cost that is now within reach and steadily dropping.

The powerful functionality is based on several features:

- *Two-way interactive communication.* The Internet supports distance learning, whereby students communicate with teachers (or technology), as easily as it enables learning where teachers communicate to students. Generally, students learn better from interactive courseware than from one-way instruction. Of course, if desired, TV-style distance-learning lectures can readily be simulated on the Internet.
- *On-demand communication protocol.* Courseware is accessed on the Internet whenever the user wants it, and from wherever the student plugs in his or her machine. No need to remember when an instructional show is on, or even to set the VCR.
- *Wide communication bandwidth.* Recent advances in compression, coupled with innovative ways to use existing infrastructure (new modems that transform TV cable into full-duplex computer connections, and ISDN as well as ADSL for copper phone wire) will make roughly the capacity of two-way video available to most Internet users.

Costs are dropping for several reasons:

- *Hardware needed for Internet access is dropping quickly in price.* In 1995 Web access required at least a low-end PC; less than two years later, "Internet appliances" such as WebTV (http://www.webtv.net) permit Web surfing at about the cost of a television plus monthly cable charges.
- *Network costs are dropping to zero.* Or, more precisely, the cost of using the Internet is low and independent of distance, so it should be just as cheap to access distance-learning material from New Zealand as from next door. (This is why more and more people are using the Internet for their telephone service, to the consternation of long-distance phone companies.)
- *De facto standards are making it easier to develop sharable courseware.* The WWW is rooted in a few document and communication protocols to which most homepage builders (or, more generally, publishers) currently adhere to. This may not make it easier to build any single distance-learning product, but, in the long run, it will help the community as a whole create better courseware.

Figure 2.4—Is the Internet the Medium of Choice for Distance Learning?

VIDEO ON THE INTERNET

In some ways, Web TV resembles on-demand video systems that some companies already use for training videos and inspirational messages from above. Indeed, it might even be better. One failing of corporate video systems has been the need for a user to download the video from an archival computer (known as a server), store it on the receiving computer (the client), and then "decompress" it before being able to play it back with special viewing software—a process taking anything from ten minutes to a few hours. With Web TV it should be possible simply to click and watch.

SOURCE: *The Economist,* January 20, 1996, p. 83.

Figure 2.5—The Internet As a Higher-Functionality, Lower-Cost Way to Deliver Video-on-Demand

Figure 2.6.) If this promise is realized, the much-heralded-but-never-accomplished "500 channels of cable TV" finally could turn into something really useful. And, because they require no new and costly infrastructure development, wireless connections, such as

CABLE MODEM TRIAL DEEMED SUCCESSFUL

A marketing trial of high-speed cable modem service conducted by Time Warner subsidiary Paragon Cable has shown virtually no churn among its 200 test participants and the waiting list is still about 300 customers long. "There's a real business here," concludes Paragon's general manager. Elmira, NY, cable customers paid a $30 installation charge and a $25 fee to receive Zenith modem units that provided access to a local database and to the Internet. Building on their success, Paragon plans to take the service commercial in Elmira at the end of March, and Time Warner is scouting out other likely locations for pilot programs. *(Broadcasting & Cable,* January 29, 1996 , p. 48)

SOURCE: Edupage, January 30, 1996.

NOTE: Edupage can be accessed at http://www.educom.edu/. Select Publications, then select Edupage from the available links. Select the desired issue by its date.

Figure 2.6—Internet Access at the Cost of Cable TV Connection

DirectPC (http://www.helius.com/), may be the most promising of all. In short, the technical problems facing the installation of inexpensive wide-bandwidth Internet connections are all but solved; the policy barriers, however, loom large, as we discuss in Chapter Six.

In addition to reducing educational costs, the shrinking price of delivering Internet-based distance learning should help address other challenges for higher education. For one thing, Internet-based distance learning could be conveniently accessible to many different kinds of learners. Part of this improved access simply means putting more people in touch with more learning resources. A new wave of cheap "Internet appliances" (dumb terminals dedicated to Web browsing) should bring Internet access within almost anyone's budget; anyone who can afford Nintendo should be able to afford the WWW.[3] And once on the Internet, all resources are equally inexpensive to browse, whether they happen to be on a homepage next door or thousands of miles away. Equally important for improved access is the ability of Internet distance learning to reach consumers at any place and any time. This flexibility will be especially important, for example, to workers who want to "retool" skills at night while working during the day.

Reflection: The Death of Distance As a Barrier to Learning

At the broadest level, an Internet style of learning or instruction delivery will, we believe, be so common that it makes little sense to view distance learning as a special form of education delivery. Since Internet and Web tools will continue to drop in cost and increase in functionality for the foreseeable future, technology should, over time, displace more and more faculty labor. Further, what labor cannot be displaced will at least not have to be nearby: The Internet can connect students with faculty and peers as easily as it connects learners with multimedia documents. Eventually, then, most learn-

---

[3]Although dropping technology costs will make the Web accessible to make many, it may be still beyond the means of many urban poor—a group who arguably might benefit most from access to low-cost educational services. As of 1993, only 7 percent of households in the bottom quartile in income owned a computer. Further, recurring Internet connection costs (still at least $20 per month in 1998) are substantial. See How Will Individual Learners Access Internet-based Education? below and, especially, Anderson, Bikson, et al. (1995) for further discussion of these access issues.

ing will be distance-independent, and the special cases will be those that are geographically bound.

Perhaps more to the point, distance learning should be viewed as a common tool in higher education, not as a separate—and esoteric—option. And most courses should be designed to use distance learning in some capacity, and often in a variety of capacities. A wide range of experiments in distance learning are already under way, and they come in many forms, rather than all fitting one mold. (See Figure 2.7.) The degree to which direct interactions are replaced can vary significantly: Telecommunications are sometimes little more than an add-on to classroom lectures; conversely, taped lectures may be the centerpiece of instruction, with face-to-face tutoring serving as a supplement; in still other cases, all discussion happens at a distance.

There is no single, obvious way to order courses from light to heavy users of distance-learning technology. Some courses that are, for example, offered exclusively at a distance (no face-to-face interaction) still make less use of telecommunication connections than classes that also include some direct contact. We ordered the following list roughly from courses that provide narrow connectivity, overall, to those that provide rich interactions. The list in Figure 2.7 is only illustrative; many distance-learning courses already mix and match features and functionality in ways we do not include here.

Less obviously, examples also differ in the bandwidth of communication, as well as the degree of interactivity. Early distance-learning courses (through postal mail) trafficked only in text, and a single interchange required days, if not weeks—not at all interactive by today's standards. Videotaped lectures distributed from a centralized source offer much greater bandwidth but no more interactivity; on the other hand, e-mail discussions between teachers and students are highly interactive but narrow in bandwidth. Some of the newest Internet-based distance learning enjoys both broadband, multimedia connections and real-time interactions, often linking not only faculty with students, but students with one another and with shared online resources. While earlier distance-learning models delivered knowledge from a centralized teacher (or "server") to students through narrow, slow, and separate connections, newer models look

Features and Functionality	*Examples*
- low bandwidth, non-interactive technology; no face-to-face contact	-Pittman's correspondence courses on shorthand in the 1840s
- high bandwidth, non-interactive technology; no face-to-face contact	-The Teaching Company (see Figure 2.10) video and audio tapes, augmented by written course material
- low- to mid-bandwidth, non-interactive technology; some face-to-face contact	-early courses from the Open University (see Figure 2.2), mainly based on paper materials, and telephone and face-to-face tutoring
- high-bandwidth, non-interactive technology; some face-to-face contact (tutoring supplements distance learning)	-many corporate training courses using "Web TV" (see Figure 2.5) are centered on on-demand multimedia courseware, but also include on-site discussions
- high-bandwidth, non-interactive technology; extensive face-to-face interaction (distance learning supplements traditional)	-many satellite- and TV-based distance- learning courses, for which classes are planned around regularly scheduled broadcasts -some World Lecture Hall classes; courseware is put online as an adjunct
- high-bandwidth, interactive technology; some face-to-face contact (tutoring supplements distance learning)	-some asynchronous learning courses (see Figure 2.8); students near a campus may come to on-site tutorials
- low-bandwidth, interactive technology; connectivity among students and distributed resources, as well as among teachers; no face-to-face contact	-educational MUDs or MOOs (see Figure 2.9), where collections of learners (mentors and students) engage in text-based dialogues in real-time and construct textual "worlds"
- high-bandwidth, interactive technology; fully connected community (teachers, students, resources, and experts); no face-to-face contact (or optional)	-newer Internet-based course from the Open University (http://www.open.ac.uk/), where face-to-face tutoring can be replaced by online tutoring and e-mail -many courses offered at virtual universities such as Athena (see Figure 4.4)

Figure 2.7—Near and Far: The Many Forms of Distance Learning

much more like an electronic community, tying together students, faculty, and distributed tools in a rich, speedy web of digital contacts.

With so many variants, it is no surprise that what makes an application of information technology an instance of distance learning is becoming less and less clear. For example, courseware such as the chemistry curriculum in the World Lecture Hall might be used in a distance-learning class; but right now, it is simply online material for an on-campus course. However, merely by skipping lectures and labs and relying on the rich Web documents to compensate for reduced in-person contact, individual students may turn it into a virtual distance-learning course. Such individual experiments, which probably have gone on informally for decades, now are leading to large-scale studies that will try to gauge the importance of distance as a barrier to learning in technology-intensive courses. (See Figure 2.8.)

It is useful to view this increasing freedom from spatial location in terms of the progressive "unbundling" of teaching functions in higher education as educational technologies have changed across time. Centuries ago, when knowledge was conveyed exclusively through an oral tradition, location was everything. With the advent of written texts, students were freed from the need to attend lectures (logically, but not always legally); however, other important functions, including tutoring, counseling, and evaluation, remained essentially face-to-face activities.

Now, just as books (and cars) have weakened the links between distance and learning in the past, today new information technologies can almost break them. Since the Internet can connect students with

> The Alfred P. Sloan Foundation is funding research on asynchronous learning networks (ALN) as part of its Learning Outside the Classroom program (http://w3.scale.uiuc.edu/education/ALN.new.html). Courses are used by students at varying distances from campus—living on campus, within commuting distance, or very far away. Two of the questions being examined by different projects are
>
> - How well do students learn as a function of distance from the physical classroom?
> - How do students' learning practices differ as a function of distance?

Figure 2.8—Does Distance Matter in Asynchronous Learning Environments?

teachers as easily as it connects students with course material, tutoring and counseling can be (and are) done through e-mail and real-time chat rooms. (See Figure 2.4.) Similarly, as reference materials increasingly become available in digital form, students will no longer need proximity to libraries. Evaluation and assessment also can be done at a distance. Written products, such as essays, already are created routinely with word processors; sending them across a network for grading can be easier than printing them and walking them into a professor's office. Multiple-choice as well as short-answer tests have been computerized for years. In a pinch, even timed, closed-book exams could be conducted using simple keystroke logging or more-sophisticated Internet video products such as CU-SeeMe (http://cu-seeme.cornell.edu/) for proctoring.

Again, the point is not that learning *should* be conducted at a distance, just that creative applications make distance less and less of a barrier to learning. The challenge will be to discover the most effective applications of distance-learning technology and to blend them together with traditional face-to-face transactions.

INCREASING QUALITY AND PRODUCTIVITY

While many applications of information technology in education try to reduce costs, others focus on the output side of the productivity equation: helping students learn more or better, or to learn new skills—applications rarely included in higher-education curricula. A collection of examples (Figure 2.9) illustrates several ways in which information-technology applications could lead to better learning and teaching outcomes.

CAI and CBT

As discussed, most successful computer-aided instruction and computer-based training applications boast of cost reductions (Figure 2.1), but a few also claim gains in the quality of student learning. Some of these applications rely on distinctly cutting-edge technology, making lavish use of multimedia, and engaging students in highly interactive discussions. However, other ideas are surprisingly simple. For example, The Teaching Company (TTC) thinks that the videotapes and audiotapes it offers can help college students improve grades in everything from history to psychology to physics. Of course, these tapes lack the interactivity of a good tutoring session, but TTC is gambling that the quality of its tapes will more than compensate: The lectures are delivered by elite, "superstar" faculty in each field, not by merely competent professors.

Some very positive reviews of these products (Figure 2.10) may be too optimistic. However, in the future, Web technology could clearly

Computer-based applications that change learning qualitatively come in various types. We order these, very roughly, from those that help students learn concepts more effectively to applications that change the kinds of ideas students learn, and how they learn them.

System/Study	*Quantitative/Qualitative Learning Results*
CAI and CBT	
Fletcher (meta-analysis of 47 studies) (1989)	-.50 standard deviations improvement in achievement (IVD technology, averaged across higher education and military training)
Kulik (review of many studies and 12 meta-analyses) (1994)	-overall small increases in learning, across academic, adult learning, and training settings (CBT technology)
The Teaching Company, http://real.org/members/listing/general/2048.22ab (video and audiotapes) (1996)	-as of May 1996, mainly testimonials about dramatic learning enhancements attributable to use of "superstar" tapes
Intelligent Tutoring Systems	
SHERLOCK (Katz et al., 1993)	-provides the equivalent of 4 years of on-the-job training in electronic troubleshooting in 20 to 30 hours
ACT tutors (Anderson, Corbett, et al., 1995)	-30 to 60 percent faster learning of programming skills, 30 to 40 percent higher scores on tests -one-grade (e.g., C to B) improvement in geometry

Figure 2.9—Information Technology and Quality Learning
(continued on next page)

Interactive Learning Environments

Apple's Classrooms of Tomorrow (ACOT) schools (Dwyer, 1994)	-studies show students wrote better, completed units in math more rapidly -by the end of 4 years, students changed how they did work, freely employing inquiry, collaboration, and general problem-solving skills
Collaborative visualization (CoVis) project (Gomez and Gordin, 1996)	-young students were able to acquire sophisticated understanding of climate and global warming -they were also able to use high-tech visualization tools, engage in open-ended inquiries, and learn collaboratively
Massively parallel microworlds (Resnick, 1994)	-young students were able to learn about complex distributed systems using simulation models run on parallel machines -they were also able to learn general heuristics for modeling decentralized systems
MUDs, MOOs, and MUSEs multi-user real-time virtual realities; as of 1996, most still text-based chat rooms, but an increasing number on the Web have graphical interfaces (McArthur and Lewis, 1996)	-most results are anecdotal, but broadly, MUDs may help learning of: -academic skills (programming, reading, typing, writing) -metacognitive and generic skills (scientific method, learning to learn, help seeking) -personal and social skills (motivation, collaboration, trust)

Figure 2.9—(continued)

make educational packages featuring superstar instructors easier to develop and more broadly accessible, perhaps leading to significant improvements in teaching and learning productivity. Imagine, for example, a course built around master lectures, digitized and put online, and combined with complementary assignments, projects, tutorials, and group discussions—like those already found in World Lecture Hall courses. Taking this course through the Internet might not be quite the same as being there in person, which would require being a student at MIT, Stanford, or a similarly elite and pricey institution. Nonetheless, for less-fortunate students, such an online

> The Teaching Company is a for-profit business that offers more than 60 audio and video courses on a wide range of academic subjects, from science to philosophy. Most are at the college level. Their main selling point is that lectures (the courses are in very traditional delivery formats, with little support material) are taught by a "dream team" of "superstar" teachers. Almost all have first-rank U.S. university affiliations. While The Teaching Company offers no solid evidence of student learning (in fact, they provide no tests or accreditation), they do pepper their brochures with testimonials from the likes of Ted Kennedy, Orrin Hatch, and the *Los Angeles Times.*

Figure 2.10—Online Superstar Teachers: Goodbye to the Merely Good?

course could be better than an in-person course offered by a second-tier university. Here, as in other areas, information technology might lead to improvements in productivity by making truly great—not merely competent—practitioners and their performances available to almost everyone.[4]

Intelligent Tutoring Systems

While replicating outstanding teaching *performances* on video might lead to improvements in learning productivity, a much more ambitious approach is to try to capture, in software, the *reasoning* of teachers. Of course, this cannot be done just by pointing a camera at a smart talking head. Rather, the process of developing so-called intelligent tutoring systems (ITS) begins with an *expert system* —a collection of heuristic rules—that is capable of answering questions and solving problems in a given subject matter. For instance, the expert system inside a good calculus ITS would be able to solve arbitrary symbolic integration problems, and would do so in a way that ap-

---

[4]See, for example, Rosen (1981) for an economic analysis of how information technology makes great performances widely available, increases the wealth of the elite (at the expense of the merely gifted), and therefore shrinks the number of people who can make a living providing information services to a small contingent. Rosen claims that this phenomenon applies not only to entertainers and sports figures, but (to a lesser extent) to lawyers and business executives, whose range of influence and availability is expanded by modern telecommunications.

proximates how an "ideal" human mathematician would reason. The expert system in an ITS is often supplemented with a student-modeling capability, which can examine a student's reasoning, find the exact step at which he or she went astray, try to diagnose the reasons for the error, and even suggest ways of overcoming the impasse.

The potential value of such highly intelligent systems is obvious. Indeed, for decades, the idea of supplying students with their own automated tutor, capable of tailoring learning experiences to students' needs at a fine level, has been the holy grail of teaching technology—with good reason. Many studies have shown that one-on-one tutoring is the best way to learn. And, as the examples in Figure 2.9 demonstrate, for a few academic subjects, ITS have nearly matched the capabilities of their human-tutor counterparts, helping to raise students' scores one letter grade or more.

However, while such systems show that ITS can raise the output side of the productivity equation in education, their successes to date are very limited. Because they try to embed detailed human-reasoning skills, both in subject-matter areas and in teaching expertise, they rely on advances in cognitive theory and software engineering. But these disciplines have yielded a detailed understanding of thinking in only a very few well-defined subjects; consequently, ITS currently are confined to relatively simple parts of algebra, geometry, computer programming, physics, and other sciences.

In higher education, then, ITS probably would be most appropriate in basic freshman and remedial classes. And, needless to say, even in these subjects, automated tutors come nowhere near the ability to mimic superstar teachers. On the contrary, ITS are frequently called "brain damaged" by most computer scientists, their developers included. Over time, however, ITS will get smarter and smarter. Buttressed by advances in cognitive science, they will capture an increasing share of human-teaching expertise, and they will extend to a wider range of subjects.

However, all evidence suggests progress here will be slow. While the speed of computer hardware continues roughly to double every two years, the intelligence of computer software, however you measure it, creeps ahead at a snail's pace.[5] But this does not mean that information technology is destined to play only a minor role in helping improve the quantity and quality of learning in higher education. It just means that some of the most obvious ways in which technology attempts to partially replace faculty as lecturers or tutors in a traditional classroom setting may not be the most promising ways, at least in the short run.

Interactive Learning Environments

A glance back at Figure 2.9 suggests that some of the most successful applications of information technology follow a very different principle: Instead of mimicking human tutors, they provide rich, simulated environments that enable students or trainees to practice skills intensively.[6] Flight simulators, the first such learning environments, are still perhaps the most compelling ones. For decades they have been singularly effective technologies for improving the quality of pilot training. In the protective environment of a virtual cockpit, pilots can perfect difficult maneuvers, trying them over and over without fear of the deadly effects of a real-world mistake.

SHERLOCK (Figure 2.9), a descendent in spirit of these early simulators, demonstrates similarly impressive outcomes: Students can learn electronics troubleshooting and fault-diagnosis skills in less than one-tenth the time they previously required. While SHERLOCK includes some important coaching supports, the basic reason that trainees acquire skills so rapidly is simply that the system can present students with simulated problem situations that arise only rarely in the real world—namely, troubleshooting the complex hardware that diagnoses faulty F-15 avionics.

---

[5]Well-publicized successes of "man over machine," such as Deep Blue's recent win over world chess champion Gary Kasparov, are false counter-examples. Deep Blue's performance relied almost exclusively on fast computer hardware. The program uses brute-force searches and "understands" virtually nothing about the way humans play the game. It is just this kind of understanding that automated tutors must possess if they are to help humans learn.

[6]Interactive and simulation-based learning environments such as those we discuss here are certainly not the only alternatives to ITS and systems that try to be "smart" or human-like. A few, listed in Figure 2.9, take different approaches; for example, some offer new "power tools" for collaborative learning.

Trainees do not learn these troubleshooting skills very quickly in the field, because problems that might foster new knowledge naturally occur, say, once every few weeks. Using SHERLOCK, such problems can be made to order every few minutes, if necessary. More generally, this and other virtual worlds rely on the fact that one of the most powerful ways to learn is by doing; but learning-by-doing works well only if the world cooperates by providing the learner with a large number of practice cases, and cases suitable to the learner's current level of expertise. In situations where the real world cannot be easily controlled or does not readily cooperate, computers can now provide rich simulated worlds, at an arbitrarily high degree of fidelity, that can be controlled with the click of a mouse.

Such environments seem promising tools for training, but can they work in higher education? While it is relatively easy to imagine how simulated worlds might be useful in teaching concrete subjects such as electronics or even physics, it is less obvious how simulations would help in abstract or symbolic disciplines such as history, philosophy, or the social sciences. However, some innovative systems are already pointing the way. For example, CoVis (Figure 2.9), *Rebel!* (Figure 2.11), and even strategy games such as SimCity, are built on top of complex computational models that capture key features of the real-world dynamic systems underlying policy decisionmaking, weather, and historical processes. True, these models do not simulate concrete physical systems; but, at an abstract level, the conceptual systems they represent also comprise dynamic cause-and-effect relationships among a collection of variables. What a new generation of simulation-based learning environments are doing, in essence, is combining computational models of such processes with highly graphical and easy-to-manipulate "visualization" front-ends. Collectively, these environments give the learner a virtual world in which many what-if experiments can be performed.

In theory, then, just as SHERLOCK provides trainees with a large number of rich avionics cases, these simulations might present learners with, say, a series of hypothetical history scenarios, some of which may have analogs in real historical events and some not. These technologies appear very interesting, but they are also very new. Whether they can lead to the dramatic gains in the quantity of learning we find with SHERLOCK remains to be seen.

Rebel! is an interactive, exploratory simulation environment for learning history—in particular the American Revolution—by playing what-if games (e.g., "What if the British had sent over more troops?"). Using it as a stand-alone system, students start the simulation, then set certain parameters (to operationalize their questions), either by loading scenarios that define collections of values or by changing them individually. Next, the system runs, and, as simulation time steps forward, the student views the virtual world unfold in a series of graphical depictions of simulation state changes. At any point the student can interrupt the run and click interface buttons that help give a better understanding of cause and effect: what was happening, and why.

We transformed *Rebel!* from an isolated simulation (running and displaying on the same machine) into a distributed one (running on a *remote* machine, and displaying on a *local* one) using the following procedure:

- The initial homepage shows, on the local interface, a picture of the initial *Rebel!* interface (saved as a GIF file, referenced in the HTML code for the page).
- The initial page also includes a Begin button, which, when clicked, triggers a script that causes *Rebel!* to begin running on the remote machine; it also invokes a new HTML page—the initialization page.
- The initialization page allows the user to select from pre-existing scenarios and to set values for specific parameters. When the form is complete, the user clicks the Run button. This invokes a script that ships all the initialization data back to the remote machine, where the *Rebel!* process is waiting for it. On the remote machine, the simulation parameter values set by the user on the local machine are then read in, and the remote *Rebel!* simulation run actually starts.
- As the simulation runs, it periodically updates its state and writes (actually, creates on the fly) a new HTML document (representing the simulation state), and puts it into the *output file,* to be displayed on the student's local machine.
- HTTP protocol on the local machine polls the remote machine at regular intervals, looking for an updated interface document in the output file, and loads it when necessary.
- "Stop" is always one option on each reloaded document. If the student selects the Stop button, a script writes instructions to a *user input file* on the remote machine, which causes the remote simulation to suspend.
- Throughout the run, a similar protocol enables the user on the local machine to interact with the simulation on the remote one: the simulation always looks for messages in the user input file to modulate its behavior, and the Web browser on the local machine always updates its image of the simulation interface by reloading the simulation output file.

Figure 2.11—Transforming *Rebel!* from an Isolated Application to a Web Distance-Learning Tool

Internet Impact: Turning Expensive Stand-Alone Systems into Cheaper Distance-Learning Technologies

Some of the applications that promise to help raise educational productivity by improving student learning, rather than by cutting costs, are already network-based systems. In CoVis, for example, students use the Internet to communicate with distant mentors, collaborate on projects with peers, gather data from remote sites, and talk with experts in atmospheric and environmental sciences. (See also Figure 2.12.) But many of the cutting-edge applications are stand-alone systems that run on only one or a few computer platforms. For instance, one might work on a Macintosh but not on a PC. Even worse, since many of these systems are still research prototypes, they may run on only relatively high-end machines (Sun Workstations or even supercomputers, for example). All this would seem to mean that some of the most interesting new information technologies for higher education will be, for the foreseeable future, either inaccessible to most students or prohibitively expensive for schools or students to acquire.

Not necessarily. One way around this problem, again, exploits the Internet and the WWW. It is already possible for stand-alone software systems to piggyback on the near-standard protocols for creating WWW documents. In doing so, these systems can be made available very widely and relatively cheaply.

As anyone who uses the WWW knows, Web browsers and servers, unlike most software, run on a wide range of machines. The considerable complexities of making key languages (such as HTML) and protocols (such as HTTP) de facto standards are hidden from the average user, who can happily create documents that will appear on any machine just about the same as they look on his or hers.[7]

[7]The universality of Web standards such as HTML and HTTP is more fragile than it might appear. Even the simple current versions of these protocols do not run on all machines. Future versions threaten to be even less general. For one thing, different groups are extending the basic standards in many incompatible directions; for another, the pressure to develop highly interactive Web objects quickly is speeding up the pace of innovation, which works against the slow processes of achieving a broad-consensus standard. That said, the current HTML and HTTP standards are far closer to a universal standard for complex computational objects than anything we have seen before.

Technically, only WWW documents enjoy this relative machine independence. However, using scripting languages (e.g., CGI) that enable programs to be initiated on remote machines and new homepages to be created and loaded on the fly, it is possible to turn almost any piece of educational software into a distance-learning application.[8]

The cleverness needed to turn isolated software into sharable distance-learning systems on the WWW might be of technical interest to some readers. (Certainly the exercise has fascinated the authors.) But such technical subtleties miss the key point of the example: Already, the Internet and WWW permit high-powered applications that run only on high-powered machines to be accessed by students who might have available only low-end machines—and almost any kind of low-end machine, not just those that the original application developer envisioned.

The future looks even more promising, on several scores. First, as already noted, ultra-cheap Internet appliances should bring down access cost even further. Second, the protocols needed to make products widely sharable across the Internet, using almost any hardware platform, are quickly falling into place. Tricks now required to turn the WWW into an interactive medium will soon lose their appeal, primarily because new Web tools, and languages such as Java, for building "live computational objects" (it is misleading to call them "documents" any longer), will soon provide primitives that make this kind of interactivity easy to achieve rather than a challenging problem to solve.

All this may mean that higher education can have its cake and eat it too. Most of the current cutting-edge information-technology applications we reviewed promise to help students learn better or faster, or both. Improving educational productivity in this sense is clearly an important goal for higher education. But, until recently, this goal seemed at odds with others: reducing the cost of delivering education and increasing access to education by an increasingly diverse population of students. Without question, in the future, most appli-

---

[8]See Figure 2.11 for an example of how we turned *Rebel!* into a Web-based history simulation that could be run on one (high-end) machine but displayed on a variety of other (low-end) ones.

cations of technology in education that offer exciting possibilities for transforming teaching and learning will continue to be developed in corporate and university research settings on high-end machines. And these will probably remain expensive, well beyond the means of almost all students and even most higher-education departments and computer labs. However, high-bandwidth networks, coupled with increasingly standardized software languages and communication protocols, and with ever-cheaper Internet terminals, should bring these cutting-edge applications within reach of learners and teachers who do not have access to the newest and fastest technologies.

This does not mean that poor students will enjoy all the same access to technology-based learning as wealthy ones, of course. There will always be computers that offer more functionality at a higher price. And even if high-quality educational materials could be accessed by anyone on any machine at any time, nothing right now prevents providers from metering this access and charging whatever the market will bear. (Nor, necessarily, should providers be prevented. These and related policy issues will be examined in Chapter Six.) The point, however, is that information technology by itself will no longer be a significant barrier to access; if anything, the WWW and Internet should be a force toward greater access to and equity in education.

Reflection: Many Interesting Options, Many Hard Choices

Certainly information technologies do more than provide better tools with which to deliver instruction and learning materials in higher education, but such tools still dominate the field of educational technology. We have discussed (or at least pointed to) a wide range of these applications, focusing especially on those that exploit the WWW, or could do so. Stepping back from the many specifics, several general points should be emphasized.

First, it should be obvious that information technologies offer many different ways to improve instruction delivery, not just one. Looking just at distance learning, there is a rich set of options to choose from. Selecting from the different choices demands attention to the (often implicit) educational goals the technologies address. Some might help higher-education institutions reduce costs; others look better-suited to increasing access to educational resources, or to increasing the quantity, quality, or speed of student learning. Overall, the proliferation of Internet and WWW resources should steadily bring down the cost of all educational software products and services. Yet, some will be more costly than others, and a few will still be very expensive for the foreseeable future.

In general, then, it is a mistake to assume that information technology provides one or a few ways to improve learning and teaching, and it is equally wrong to believe that technology applications will affect just a single educational goal: cost reduction.

A third assumption, probably more widely believed, is also wrong: that information technology is mainly a vehicle to enhance educational productivity. Look back for a moment at the last few information-technology applications described in Figure 2.9. While some, such as SHERLOCK, clearly intend to help speed up learning, or to improve learning of well-defined subject areas, it is much less obvious how others are trying to improve educational productivity in any simple sense. Instead, they are generally trying to transform the *processes* and *products* of learning. For example, they might exploit new visualization technologies to enable junior students to learn about complex systems that previously only graduate students found comprehensible; and they might foster deeper understanding through inquiry-based learning rather than traditional lectures, or through collaborative-learning methods that simply never existed prior to high-bandwidth networks.

In short, here information technology is a driver of educational reform, not of productivity enhancement—unless *productivity* is redefined to include a wide range of qualitative changes, not just quantitative improvements.

That these applications *transform* processes and products of learning more than they *enhance* productivity has several implications for their adoption, implementation, and costs. Consider, from the point of view of the developer, how many different facets of an educational context might need to change for the potentially impressive benefits of such applications to be realized. (See Figure 2.12.) Clearly, the technology itself—the tools actually used by students in learning—is just the tip of the iceberg. Other possible changes range from the roles of teachers, to methods of evaluating learning, to deeper philosophical views of how learning happens and what constitutes knowledge.

Here is what the CoVis researchers say about their project and goals (http://www.covis.nwu.edu/info/CoVis_OV.html):

"Traditionally, K-12 science education has consisted of the teaching of well-established facts. This approach bears little or no resemblance to the question-centered, collaborative practice of real scientists. Through the use of advanced technologies, the CoVis Project is attempting to transform science learning to better resemble the authentic practice of science. . . .

The CoVis Project will explore issues of scaling, diversity, and sustainability as they relate to the use of networking technologies to enable high school students to work in collaboration with remote students, teachers, and scientists. An important outcome of this work will be the construction of distributed electronic communities dedicated to science learning.

Participating students study atmospheric and environmental sciences through inquiry-based activities. Using state of the art scientific visualization software, specially modified to be appropriate to a learning environment, students have access to the same research tools and data sets used by leading-edge scientists in the field.

The CoVis Project provides students with a range of collaboration and communication tools. These include: desktop video teleconferencing; shared software environments for remote, real-time collaboration; access to the resources of the Internet; a multimedia scientist's "notebook"; and scientific visualization software. In addition to deploying new technology, we work closely with teachers at participating schools to develop new curricula and new pedagogical approaches that take advantage of project-enhanced science learning. "Collaborative Visualization" thus refers to development of scientific understanding which is mediated by scientific visualization tools in a collaborative context. The CoVis Project seeks to understand how science education could take broad advantage of these capabilities, providing motivating experiences for students and teachers with contemporary science tools and topics."

— * —

Figure 2.12—What It Might Take to Make CoVis Work
(continued on next page)

Here are a few of the transformations in traditional classroom practice needed to realize these goals:

- *Philosophy of learning and teaching.* Learning is no longer viewed as absorbing information but constructing meaning (instructionism vs. constructionism); inquiry rather than drill-and-practice is the preferred means of acquiring knowledge; and visualization as well as text-based comprehension is a key approach to understanding.
- *Teachers' roles (and training).* Teachers act as mentors and guides to information resources, rather than as lecturers and sole sources of knowledge; they also must be fluent with new collaboration and visualization technologies.
- *Students' tasks.* Students learn mainly through inquiry structured by projects; most projects are done in collaboration with other students and external experts (through network connections), rather than individually.
- *Curriculum structure.* Curricula are organized around authentic projects that embed long-term tasks comparable to those tackled by professionals in the field; small-scale tasks, such as solving a collection of algebra questions, are largely abandoned..
- *Classroom organization.* Classes are organized conceptually and physically by projects and computer networks. As students conduct their inquiries, the networks connect students and their tasks to external databases and experts who are sources of information, support, and commentary. Students spend little time engaged in paperwork at desks.
- *Evaluation strategies.* Authentic evaluation strategies replace traditional ones; students are evaluated on the basis of the quality of their projects, rather than their scores on short-answer or multiple-choice tests.

Figure 2.12—(continued)

All of this is roughly consistent with a simple rule we have distilled from our own research in developing and implementing educational technology: If a technology fits into an existing educational process and tries to enhance existing educational products, you spend 75 percent of your time developing the technology and 25 percent worrying about all other implementation issues; if a technology tries to transform educational processes and products, you spend 75 percent of your time attending to these nontechnical, often complex, and frequently invisible changes in institutional practice and structure.

If anything, our 75/25 rule understates some of the complexities and costs of integrating cutting-edge applications into the classroom. True, it does suggest that deep institutional changes might be necessary to make the best use of some information technologies. However, it also seems to imply that we can anticipate the best ways to use these tools in advance, and that the biggest challenge will be to change the educational system to reflect what society knows it needs to learn and teach.

Although this statement is probably far too optimistic, who would have imagined a decade ago that visualization technologies or simulated worlds would open new educational experiences to learners? By the same token, it is extremely difficult to predict with any confidence what new and interesting applications of information technology for learning will surface over the next decade, or to imagine the kinds of institutional changes that might be necessary to best exploit these new tools.

This is not to argue that all good applications of the Internet and WWW to deliver education are shrouded in mystery. Again, there will be many options to choose from. Some applications—perhaps simple Internet distance-learning tools and the next generation of ITS—may continue to fit well into existing higher-education structures and to reduce costs or increase teacher productivity, others may give rise to new structures and cause us to rethink our ideas of educational productivity, and a few may transform learning in completely unexpected ways. Shortly, we will see additional examples of unexpected applications of information technology. Chapter Six follows up a few policy implications of this uncertainty.

Chapter Three

IMPROVING THE CREATION OF INSTRUCTION AND LEARNING MATERIALS

Information technology not only provides new options for instruction delivery, it can also help create new instruction and learning materials. (What is the point of electronic delivery if there is nothing to deliver?) In turn, these new methods and tools can address some of the key challenges for higher education, including responding more nimbly to changes in demand and competing with new providers. As before, information technology provides not one or two, but several ways of improving the development of instruction and learning materials. Some options are relatively simple extensions of current methods, while others are novel.

EXPANDING TRADITIONAL METHODS OF PRODUCTION

To simplify slightly, the traditional pipeline for producing educational materials (and intellectual artifacts, in general) has four key components:

- Authors create documents.
- Publishers mainly manufacture and market copies of these products.
- Libraries primarily acquire, store, and distribute copies of the products to the nearby community.
- Readers consume the products.

These groups have played relatively stable roles in the publication process for decades, even centuries. However, information technology is changing these roles; equally important, it is transforming the copyright and intellectual-property-rights laws that underpin relationships among the participants.

The simplest view of this change argues that new information technologies will reduce, perhaps even eliminate, the need for publishers and libraries. Historically, publishers and libraries have been essential intermediaries, enabling authors and audiences to reach one another. Authors rarely possessed the tools, skills, and capital necessary to typeset their books, calculate the size of production runs, or coordinate with vendors. By the same token, individual readers (especially students and researchers) rarely could afford to acquire vast libraries of literary holdings. Publishers and libraries have traditionally met these needs. However, as educational products become increasingly digital and networked, one line of argument goes, the latter two groups may prove unnecessary, at least from a technical perspective.

Today, academic research provides the most-impressive examples of how higher education is exploiting information technology to simplify the document-production pipeline. (This is hardly surprising, considering that, as we have already noted, the Internet was an active tool in scholarly research long before it played a significant role in instruction.) Members of several research communities in medicine, mathematics, and the physical sciences now publish their work, at least in "preprint" form, on the Internet. (See Figure 3.1.) The growth of such publications has been explosive: The first electronic academic journals came online in 1991; by mid-1995, more than 300 populated cyberspace;[1] in July 1996, according to the Association of Research Libraries,[2] there were almost 1700 electronic journals and newsletters; and estimates ballooned to over 5000 by early 1998.[3] Although individual publishers have been quick to add organization and decoration, many of these works, in their simplest form, comprise a collection of homepages that can be read at a distance using

---

[1]For an overview of electronic journals, links to many sites of and articles on electronic journals, as well as some current (as of spring 1995) statistics on their growth, see McEldowney (1995).

[2]See http://www.arl.org/scomm/edir/ for additional information and statistics; Dewar (1998) offers further discussion of the progression from manuscripts to Internet Books.

[3]See "Virtual Publishing," in *The Economist*, January 24, 1998.

Researchers have made the transition from print to bits in several steps—a process that is still continuing. In 1991 scientists at Los Alamos National Laboratory took the first step by setting up a service to distribute "e-prints" (electronic versions of paper preprints) over the Internet. Since then, their service has grown to handle over 40,000 requests per day (see http://xxx.lanl.gov/).

The next step is to put the whole journal review and publication process online. Researchers now submit their articles by e-mail or the Web, editors send them electronically to reviewers, and the final revised versions are published in an electronic journal. As a result, turnaround time for publication is now a few weeks, not months; subscription rates are usually a fraction of those of paper journals, and sometimes free. By 1995, McEldowney (1995) had found over 300 electronic journals.

A third step is just now being taken. Some sites that began as single journals are adding new publications and new functionality. BioMedNet (http://BioMedNet.com/BioMedNet/ biomed.htm), for example, offers researchers a library of publications, search services to help locate titles, job listings, and several other kinds of assistance for professionals.

(See also *The Economist,* December 16, 1995, p. 78, for information on electronic academic publication.)

Figure 3.1—Scholar As Publisher: Making Research Directly Available to Readers Across the Internet

any Web browser. Provided that you know the Internet location of an online journal, accessing the current issue (if there is one; some electronic magazines simply accumulate publications over time) is simply a matter of entering the address and reading what comes up on your screen.

This kind of publication is gaining popularity for several reasons. Cutting out the traditional publisher intermediary not only dramatically speeds up the rate at which new ideas get into "print"; it also cuts publication costs and provides a direct link to readers, who can access the papers from anywhere on the Internet as soon as they are available. The audience, in turn, is often encouraged to be publishers in return, using e-mail to send feedback and reviews on articles directly back to authors. Finally, problems of calibrating production runs, disposing of unsold inventory, and dealing with unsatisfied consumer demand simply do not arise with digital, networked publications. No longer do students and faculty need to wait for other scholars to return copies of popular books: They simply print their own copies on demand.

DIGITAL LIBRARIES: NEW MEDIA, NEW SERVICES, NEW INSTITUTIONS

If libraries existed only to store copies of books and other physical artifacts, and to share them with members of nearby communities, then the preceding examples might suggest that such institutions are in danger of extinction. Not surprisingly, traditional libraries are not ready to give up the ghost just yet. Along with publishers, whose traditional roles are similarly threatened, libraries are attempting to redefine their functions in ways that maintain roles for them in the delivery of information in digital, networked environments.

New digital libraries can try to go beyond being paperless versions of traditional libraries in at least three ways. First, freed of the need to store copies of (sometimes rare) documents, they can focus more on services that will help students and faculty find and organize information in vast virtual collections. Second, freed of the need to maintain collections in locations physically near their communities of readers, they can plan to aggregate virtual holdings into more encompassing, complete, and up-to-date collections. And, third, freed of the dominance of static print (audio and video can be digitized as readily as can typed text), digital libraries can grapple with the complexities of representing and cataloguing new multimedia documents.

A number of projects are engaged in the important, but painfully slow, translation of paper products into digital form. Project Gutenberg (http://gutenberg.etext.org/), for example, aims to have 10,000 texts online by the year 2001; with a growing network of volunteers, it is now downloading about eight new titles per month. The project's mission is to provide universal access to texts. For this reason, it is digitizing only materials in the public domain, and it is using the most basic storage format: "plain vanilla ASCII."

Already today, then, a student using almost any computer coupled to the Internet can read the complete works of Shakespeare. The National Digital Library (http://lcweb.loc.gov/homepage/new.html), part of the Library of Congress, has used its considerable resources to digitize several hundred thousand Library holdings. Not limited to simple text, these holdings range from documents of the Continental Congress, to turn-of-the-century films, to Matthew Brady's Civil War photographs. Many students and scholars are even now making serious use of the Library's historical collections, reference materials, and search tools.

Tools to Find and Organize Information

As impressive as these conversion efforts are, though, even a quick scan of the burgeoning literature on digital libraries shows that most of the action is elsewhere. Few of the universities funded through the Digital Libraries Initiative (sponsored jointly by the National Science Foundation [NSF], the Defense Advanced Research Projects Agency [DARPA], and the National Aeronautics and Space Administration [NASA)]), for instance, have yet to build or acquire substantial digital holdings. Rather, they are developing tools and software agents with which digital libraries can be constructed and can be effectively searched by students, faculty, and researchers. (See Figure 3.2.)

To anyone who has browsed the WWW—which itself can be viewed as a vast and unorganized digital library—the need for these search and management tools is obvious. Most of the information available on the Internet today is of questionable quality, at best. As holdings merge, it will become more and more difficult to find high-quality products, let alone products relevant to a chosen topic. Even more problematic, traditional tools for managing this search probably will not help much in new digital libraries. Quite aside from the fact that traditional schemes barely work even today (card catalogs and huge cross-referencing tomes almost always seem to need the skills of experienced librarians), these print-indexing tools simply do not scale up well to multimedia documents that include several varieties of visual and auditory materials, as well as text. The hope is that a new generation of digital library tools and software agents will be able to

Subject matter/content:

The content will emphasize a diverse collection, focused on earth and space sciences, which can satisfy the needs of many different types of users. The content will be supplied by publishers, although the project will eventually allow all users to publish their work. A related project, the Journal Storage Project (JSTOR), will digitize and make available all issues from the first publication through 1990 of ten economics journals to the NSF-UMDL.

Testbed description:

The UMDL will consider a complex array of technical and socioeconomic issues and will focus the research through the design, construction, and evaluation by real users of a testbed system. The testbed will consist of a cooperating set of three types of software agents: user interface agents, mediation agents, and collection agents.

User interface agents will conduct interviews with users to establish their needs such as what they need to know, and the breadth and depth of the information they require. The interface agent will also enable the user to specify areas of interest so that the system can notify the user of items of potential relevance.

Mediation agents will coordinate searches of many distinct but networked collections by taking orders from the interface agents. This will allow the user to search many libraries simultaneously in ways that meet time, relevancy, and economic constraints. The mediation agents will depend upon a conspectus that describes the contents of the various collections on the network.

Collection interface agents are associated with each specific collection and can handle searching within specific collections of text, images, graphics, audio and video. Information held in the collections may be owned by various entities, some of which may demand some control over dissemination of contents or compensation for access to their copyrighted material. The system design will provide mechanisms to protect information access and support remuneration operations.

The users of the digital library testbed will include expert researchers, students, and the general public. The library will include media types ranging from page images to interactive, compound documents and eventually real-time interaction with data. Critical to the exploitation of these resources will be ongoing programs of evaluation, training, user assistance, and outreach.

SOURCE: Excerpted from http://www.si.umich.edu/UMDL/intro.html on February 22, 1998.

Figure 3.2—Providing Services to Manage Information in Digital Libraries

understand multimedia documents, and that they will be as easy to use as they are powerful. Some of these tools are little more than user-friendly search engines, which find titles through keyword searches. But others might fulfill, in electronic form, many of the roles of a personalized library assistant or online note-taker. (See Figure 3.2.)

Aggregating Single Libraries into Mega-Libraries

Another way in which libraries are trying to grow beyond their paper counterparts is simply to merge holdings. Such aggregation rarely happens in traditional libraries: One-of-a-kind documents are closely guarded and are regarded as highly limited resources that curators are naturally reluctant to part with; the cost of moving, recataloguing, and repositioning artifacts usually is prohibitive; and merging libraries into a centralized location threatens to reduce access to materials by many readers in the affected communities.

Access to materials in digital libraries, by contrast, is independent of distance, so merging can only add to the resources available to communities. Moreover, merging digital holdings is comparatively trivial. Sometimes, libraries can be merged just by adding a few well-placed menu items, and smart search tools can overcome many of the resulting duplications that may arise from such mergings. (For example, duplicate finds, or "hits," can be automatically eliminated before search results are presented to the student.) And, if mergers are planned a little more carefully at the outset (also often aided by digital merging and interface-building tools), users can be presented an interface with the look and feel of a single digital "mega-library" rather than a collection of smaller ones, each with a different interaction protocol.

Today, even the largest digital libraries are small; while the Library of Congress houses over 100 million "traditional" artifacts, its online counterpart, the National Digital Library, "houses" a few hundred thousand, at most. When digital libraries finally acquire substantial holdings, they will have promise for addressing several important goals and problems of higher education, the first being costs. Costs could drop substantially. From a technical perspective, a document need cost no more than the price of producing it on a nearby high-quality laser printer, which would easily undercut the price of common university texts, not to mention rare volumes. Of course, publishers are unlikely to tolerate such indiscriminate copying of their property, at least as copyright law now stands. However, by aggregating their acquisitions, digital college libraries are already discovering that they can use their coordinated buying power to negotiate much more effective licensing deals than publishers are willing to offer on books. (See Figure 3.3.)

Digital libraries can improve access to educational material even as they reduce access cost, thereby promising to be a key component in future distance-learning curricula. Students within a university will enjoy better access to digital materials, in part because they will be able to use them at any place and any time, not just in library study halls; and they will not have to wait for days or weeks until popular titles are returned to the shelf. More interestingly, as digital libraries merge, students can access the very best materials, regardless of their institutional affiliation.

Even if such mergers do not happen officially, students may be able to implement them informally. Today, for example, nothing prevents University of Michigan students on the Web from accessing

LIBRARIANS, UNITE—FOR BUYING POWER

College librarians are banding together to purchase electronic resources for their institutions. "We've found that this sort of group purchasing power has really enabled us to leverage the dollars that we have and to get resources we couldn't have otherwise," says an associate librarian at the University of Texas at Austin, which buys publications through the TexShare consortium. The group buying arrangement is also advantageous for publishers, who don't need to spend as much on marketing: "As a group, we'll pay the vendor more money than they can realistically get by slogging it out school by school," says the executive director of OhioLINK, which includes more than 40 colleges and universities. The president of Britannica Online figures that more than half of the 293 institutions using his product are doing so under consortium-based licenses. (*Chronicle of Higher Education,* February 9, 1996, p. A21)

SOURCE: Edupage, February 11, 1996.

Figure 3.3—Bigger Is Better?

digital holdings at Stanford, MIT, University of Illinois, or any of the other dozens of online libraries. For that matter, nothing prevents any Internet user—say, an unemployed worker in Detroit or a teenager in Harlem—from perusing these digital documents.

This may not be true for long, however. It is quite easy for universities to put up "firewalls," which permit access only to their students and faculty. Technically easy, yes, but perhaps hard to justify; digital-library resources, unlike books, are simply not "consumed" when used. With well-designed library servers and ample bandwidth, the hundreds of authorized users of a digital library should not notice a thousand or more unofficial users.

All of this would suggest that the best world of all would be one with a single digital library, located at a single site (or perhaps distributed throughout cyberspace), and surrounded by a collection of smart, user-friendly, library tools and software agents to help find digital resources, piece them together into new documents, and share them among students and faculty. If bigger is better, why stop at merging just a few digital collections?

Obstacles to Building Productive Digital Libraries

For several reasons, this vision of the future is a long way off, even if it is a good one. To begin with, different universities and different communities may simply want to retain different digital documents; local decency laws, as well as informal cultural preferences, will continue to encourage diversity, and sometimes insularity, in digital holdings. Even discounting regional preferences, some important technical hurdles still need to be overcome.

A completely universal digital library presupposes standards for representing the different kinds of multimedia information that make up the digital documents. The de facto standards for WWW homepages (namely, HTML and HTTP) are a good first step in this direction, but they are a long way from being complete. Indeed, closure may be a receding goal, because new data formats and media types are being spawned faster than standards for existing ones are being settled. It is also important to remember that few of the artifacts now in traditional libraries (so-called legacy materials) have been digitized; they must be included in any digital library that even pretends to supplant a paper-based one. On top of all this, digital materials, no less than paper products, are subject to decay and deterioration (Rothenberg, 1995).

Although the technical problems are substantial, perhaps the biggest obstacles to building digital libraries are legal and institutional. Higher-education institutions have a long history of independence in the way they provide services. Even if economic and social arguments point toward merging digital libraries, whether universities will enthusiastically embrace changes that might threaten their institutional identity is not clear—especially if they can convince themselves that sharing their knowledge base will lose students, and thus revenue, to competing schools.

Finally, copyright problems could kill the development of digital libraries in their infancy. Over decades, copyright law has forged a delicate balance between the interests of publishers and those of consumers, with libraries in the middle. First-sale doctrine permits libraries to lend books without requiring libraries or readers to further compensate publishers and authors. Similarly, over time, libraries have negotiated extensions of fair-use laws that allow students and faculty to (photo)copy materials without violating copyright. Current copyright law is not particularly generous to consumers, and a direct application of it to digital documents, if possible at all, would certainly not give readers the more-or-less free and unlimited copying privileges that are tacitly assumed in the scenarios we just sketched.

But even these rules would be preferable to some of the revisions of copyright now being drafted with digital materials in mind. The 1994 "Green Paper" put out by the Clinton administration's Intellectual Property Working Group, for example, would require readers to pay by use: Each time a copyrighted digital document was copied—including (the publishers hope) copies cached on a local machine whenever a document is browsed on the Web—publishers would be compensated. If these kinds of changes are enacted, students and faculty will be required to pay each time they skim virtual shelves that hold recent issues of digital periodicals. Far from looking like progress, this future could be a big step backward in public access to knowledge: How many university libraries charge admission to their reading rooms? Cyberspace-savvy academics fear, with good reason, that digital libraries will never thrive if copyright law is rewritten to be balanced so heavily in favor of publishers. (See Figure 3.4.)

HIGHER ED GROUPS EYE ELECTRONIC COPYRIGHT BILL

Representatives from higher education associations testified last week before a House subcommittee, urging lawmakers not to pass new electronic copyright rules before their impact on colleges and universities can be assessed. At issue is a revised definition of "fair use" of copyrighted digital materials that threatens to eliminate or severely restrict online interlibrary loans, and would also prevent professors from using such materials as part of their courses. *(Chronicle of Higher Education,* February 16, 1996, p. A26*)*

SOURCE: Edupage, February 18, 1996.

Figure 3.4—Higher Education's Fight with New Electronic Copyright Laws

DIGITAL PUBLISHERS: JUMPING INTO THE FUTURE OR HOLDING ONTO THE PAST?

Publishers, of course, see the threat very differently. To them, the Internet calls up their ultimate nightmare: The U.S. Library of Congress buys one copy of a digital text for its collection, makes the copy available on interlibrary loan to any other library or patron (just as libraries generally do today), whereupon, since bits are so easily reproduced, every reader can manufacture his or her own copy with a few mouse clicks. In this scenario, the first sale of a digital book might well be the last. While admittedly fanciful, this extreme example holds more than a grain of truth. Copyright law can afford to be more generous when built-in barriers—the machinery needed to reproduce tapes, the time and cost of photocopy paper, for instance—provide natural disincentives to duplication. But these disincentives are largely gone with digital products. So, today, most publishers spend as much time defending themselves against the Internet as they do creating products for it. (See Figure 3.5.)

BOOK PUBLISHERS WORRY OVER THREAT OF INTERNET

Publishers may not be feeling panic, but they are clearly edgy about the prospects of new technology, which many consider as potentially significant as Gutenberg's development of moveable type.

Their chief concern is the improvement of computer technology that will make it easier and faster to scan books.

In statements to the House Subcommittee on Courts and Intellectual Property Rights, the Association of American Publishers fretted about a new world: "although not wanting to be melodramatic, publishers do fear for their future, and the well-being of their authors, when looking at a world with low-cost, easy-to-use ubiquitous scanners, copiers and binders."

The publishers group commissioned several studies on the issue, including one that concluded that there is no practical way to "unilaterally prevent" unauthorized distribution of books.

Instead the association is pressing for methods to detect copyright violations with a "uniform file identifier system."

It is essentially a license plate on copyrighted work that contains the publisher's name and the identity of the person who purchased the work. The publishing industry is backing legislation before the House and Senate to make it a criminal and civil offense to alter these cyber license plates. Even they are not quite sure what form the identifying codes will take, but they do know they want them.

SOURCE: New York Times on the Web, *CyberTimes,* March 18, 1996.

Figure 3.5—Who Wins: Publishers, Readers, Both, or Neither?

Over the past few years, this fear has slowly started to transform through a variety of other emotions and actions: uncertain acceptance (Figure 3.6, panel 1), careful study (Figure 3.6, panel 2), strategic mergers (Figure 3.6, panel 3), and hasty exits (Figure 3.6, panel 4). Still, recognizing a booming educational software market whose retail sales may have climbed as much as 50 percent in 1995 (to over $500 million), traditional publishing houses, together with some fresh competitors, are beginning to sell substantial quantities of new products to higher education.

PUBLISHERS WARILY EYE THE NET

Members of the Association of American Publishers have decided that they must become actively involved in the deployment of online information distribution systems, or get left behind in the dust. Up until now, worries over rampant unauthorized dissemination have resulted in "significant hesitation about investing" in electronic publishing, says the chairman of the AAP's Enabling Technologies Committee. Now, they've decided to try to resolve copyright issues "before copyright infringement on the network becomes very widespread and assumed to be the way the network works. It's a recognition that whereas in the past, publishing members of the AAP have been able to leave technological concerns to suppliers—such as compositors, typesetters and printers—in networkpublishing we cannot leave it to others."

SOURCE: *Chronicle of Higher Education*, June 23, 1995, p. A18.

COLLEGE TEXTBOOKS—PAST HISTORY?

Publishing CEOs to Address the Future of College Textbooks at ConTEXT '96. With the increasing presence of distance learning programs, custom-made course packs, and multimedia tools in higher education, the future form of learning materials remains a big question. To address some of these issues, chief executives from three publishing companies will share their insights and ideas on the future direction of the textbook publishing industry during ConTEXT '96: A Conference on Textbooks and Technology.

SOURCE: EDUCOM UPDATE, January 15, 1996.

LEARNING COMPANY PREFERS BRODERBUND TO SOFTKEY

The Learning Company has accepted a new merger offer from Broderbund, rejecting a rival offer from Softkey, the Cambridge, Mass.-based company that has little regard for the Learning Company's management. A top Broderbund executive says, "We believe that the management of the Learning Company is one of its key assets. We're looking at a merger with a successful company that is doing a lot of things right. The last thing we want to do is alter that chemistry."

SOURCE: *New York Times,* November 9, 1995, p. C3.

MURDOCH SELLS EDUCATIONAL PUBLISHING GROUP

Rupert Murdoch's News Corporation is selling HarperCollins Publishing to the U.K.-based media conglomerate Pearson PLC. A Smith Barney analyst says that "Educational publishing doesn't fit News Corp.'s image as a global distributor of information. Rupert has a lot of different objectives, and this is not one of them." Pearson PLC will now rank fourth in educational book publishing, behind McGraw Hill, Macmillan, and Harcourt-Brace.

SOURCE: *New York Times,* February 10, 1995, p. 19.

Figure 3.6—Traditional Publishers and the Digital Enemy: Fight or Flight?

Conservatism, however, still seems the order of the day, in at least two senses. First, the initial reaction of many large publishers has been to simply follow the lead of the pioneering academics, who are abandoning paper journals in favor of just-in-time electronic versions (Figure 3.7), following the "if you can't beat them, buy them" strategy: Some small and informal online publishing sites are being acquired by professional publishers. BioMedNet (Figure 3.1), for example, initially the brain-child of a few researchers, was taken over by Current Science, a small but fast-moving new publishing firm that specializes in value-added electronic products. Second, while publishers certainly will develop more and better digital products for higher education—BioMedNet has grown from a single digital journal to a rich, online community, for example—the processes by which new titles are created in the future probably will not be much different from what they are now.

To find places where information technology is changing the ways in which learning materials are created in a big way, we must look at a much smaller scale: the individual publisher.

MCGRAW-HILL PLANS ELECTRONIC ACADEMIC PUBLISHING

McGraw-Hill, the publishing and information services company, is considering the development of electronic academic journals that could be published more quickly and economically than traditional academic journals. An enthusiast about information technology, McGraw-Hill chairman Joseph Dionne says: "If you take this technology, you have someone submit his research, have it reviewed by knowledgeable people, the process could be done in a week or two weeks." He says he has approached such groups as the Society of Physics and the Society of Chemistry, and "there is a very real possibility that it is going to happen over the next five years." (*Financial Times,* October 16, 1995, p. 19)

SOURCE: Edupage, October 17, 1995.

Figure 3.7—Paper Publishing Elephants Following Digital Mice?

INTERNET IMPACT: INNOVATIVE WAYS TO CREATE NEW INSTRUCTION AND LEARNING MATERIALS

Consider again the World Lecture Hall, a virtual repository of online course materials. We discussed in Chapter Two how specific courses here might be part of a new generation of distance-learning class materials. But we look now at the Hall itself, rather than at its constituent products (Figure 3.8), to see how new instruction and learning materials are created.

The most prominent feature of the Hall is a large table that organizes specific courseware by subject matter. It is much like a standard university course catalog, except that the offerings are full sets of course materials, rather than brief course descriptions. The Hall also provides tools that allow new courses to be easily searched and added, and a "What's New" link to identify the latest entries (a very valuable resource for frequent browsers, since hundreds of courses already reside at the Hall).

The World Lecture Hall demonstrates two very powerful benefits of information technology for education—one already widely touted, the other less so. Relatively familiar is the idea that new technologies encourage individual, home-grown production. In higher education, we have seen such production in electronic journals that bypass traditional publication bottlenecks, as well as in online courses constructed by individual faculty almost from scratch, using digital materials. Outside education, the examples are often even more compelling. Today, for example, audio and video desktop publishing puts at one's fingertips the facilities that just a few years ago were available only to large, well-funded professional studios. Using these tools, small grassroots print-journalists, moviemakers, and record producers are already making significant inroads into markets traditionally dominated by big players. There is no reason to believe that, at least on technical grounds, educational publication and the creation of instructional materials will be immune to these sea changes.

The second feature has more to do with the World Lecture Hall itself, and the cooperative curriculum development it can encourage, than with the nature and origins of its constituent online courses. The Hall attempts to provide a location and supporting tools that will encourage faculty not only to create new online course materials, but to

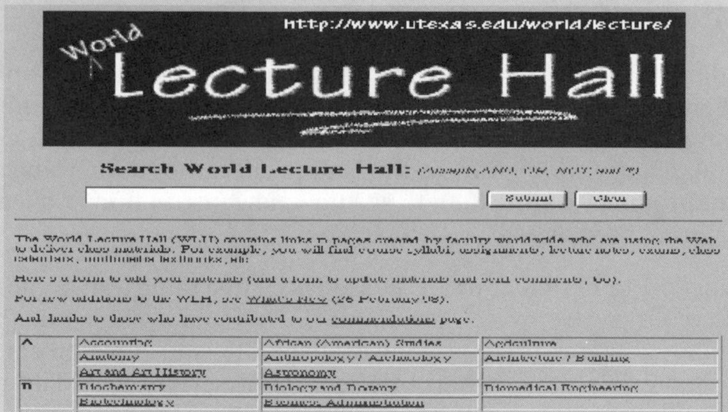

The World Lecture Hall is a Web site managed out of the University of Texas. Its main feature is a large table that organizes several hundred courses, alphabetically, by subject name. Users select a subject link, which then leads to a page listing all specific courses of that type. These course links, in turn, can be followed down to their component pieces: lecture notes, tests, and so on.

The World Lecture Hall encourages new course submissions, which may be completely original or modifications of courses already resident. However, as of 4/97, it provides relatively few tools for users or developers beyond a "What's New" link that lists recent additions, a simple search facility, and the table of course offerings itself. The Hall's developers apparently do not review courses offered by developers, follow other policies for quality control, or provide tools to help consumers find and compare products.

SOURCE: Image excerpted from http://www.utexas.edu/world/lecture on February 28, 1998.

Figure 3.8—The World Lecture Hall: Homepage Image

share those materials with others. Because the Hall is implemented as a Web homepage, all materials from a course can be downloaded (a trivial process) from the Hall site (which happens to be in Texas) to the browser's home machine. Using simple but very powerful digital cut-and-paste tools, this copy can be edited into a new course—possibly for a slightly different topic and audience, and, perhaps also a better product. In any case, the new version can be returned to the World Lecture Hall, adding to the materials available to share with the academic community. Eventually, this kind of chaotic cooperation might lead to a vast collection of digital courses of progressively better quality, as a new set of course creators stands on the shoulders of the current creators.

Challenges to Building Productive Individual Publishing Communities in Higher Education

How likely is this rosy future? On the one hand, early indications seem promising. It was quite possible that when the World Lecture Hall was established (in 1994), no one would have come to the site. At its inception, the Hall contained very few online courses, and so had little value to browsers. But, by late 1996, the Hall contained several hundred courses; according to its managers, dozens of offerings flow in each month, and the pace is increasing. In short, at least this communal repository of digital instructional material demonstrates what economists refer to as positive "network externalities": the more users adopt the product, the more valuable (but not more scarce) the product becomes for other users.

On the other hand, most home-grown products—whether in the form of videotapes, audio recordings, or Web homepages—suffer from a common problem: Although their creators view them as priceless, few others may. Just as once we were bored to tears by our neighbors' vacation slide shows, today most Web surfers are frustrated by the thousands (now probably millions) of homepages that serve only to hide the few gems they seek. In the case of virtual collections such as the World Lecture Hall, it is likely that if potential consumers (who may also be producers) cannot find quality digital course materials, they will cease browsing this site (and adding to it). If so, the number of new entries will decrease, and, with fewer shoulders to stand on, the overall quality of offerings is unlikely to improve quickly, if at all. In this future, the World Lecture Hall, far from flourishing, would probably disappear within a few semesters.

Whether or not such sites foster a productive community of grassroots publishing in higher education will depend on a number of factors. Luck and good timing may play a role. If, for example, home-grown sites develop strong early products, they may attract the attention and new contributors needed to sustain them through their formative period. Also, even if quality products exist, they must be easy to find. Internet search engines and smart agents already help consumers locate useful sites and ignore irrelevant ones. Providers also have several means at their disposal to simplify search and improve product quality. Passive tools, such as the World Lecture Hall's table organization and "What's New" option, help make navigation easier for consumers.

Other providers (although not the World Lecture Hall) take more active steps, preferring to control the quality of products they include in their collections, rather than just relying on consumers to cut through irrelevant materials with search tools. One ingenious, simple idea that virtual Yellow Pages (BigBook, for example, at http://www.bigbook.com/) are trying is to rely on consumer popularity to organize products and shape the market by letting users rate any business in their database and permit new buyers to see these reviews. Although this strategy has not been applied to educational courseware databases, the implementation would probably be very simple; however, the long-term consequences of using such a quality-management scheme would certainly be far from easy to predict.

Taking a more traditional approach, electronic journals such as BioMedNet have instituted formal peer-review procedures. Similarly, many of the electronic discussion groups on Usenet (the newsgroup side of the Internet) are moderated, rather than uncontrolled. Moderators can play a wide range of roles: reorganizing and packaging submitted materials, editing copy, adding commentary, and even censoring contributions outright. All this sounds very much like the value-added functions of traditional publishers. It hardly comes as a surprise, therefore, that publishing firms, seeking to redefine their roles in the digital age, are now seeking partnerships with developers of home-grown online course materials for higher education. In addition to ensuring quality and packaging of new products, many publishers are planning also to market the courseware, secure copyright agreements, and arrange licensing. (See Figure 3.9.)

UNIVERSITY ONLINE

University Online, a small Internet publisher that licenses 200 ready-made high school and college courses, is working with George Washington and George Mason Universities to create tutorials and more online courses at the higher education level, and is seeking more universities for similar alliances. The company's president is working with textbook publishers to obtain the electronic rights to their materials, and will then pay the publishers' royalties and split the tuition with the universities that license its products. (*The Wall Street Journal,* February 24, 1996, p. B5D)

SOURCE: Edupage, February 25, 1996.

Figure 3.9—Grassroots Developers and Traditional Publishers: A Marriage?

Individual publishing on the Internet is so new that it is difficult to determine how significantly it will contribute to the creation of new instruction and learning materials. If it flourishes, however, this innovative approach could speak to several important goals and problems of higher education, such as the need for just-in-time and on-demand learning.

Home-grown publishing is now technically feasible because information technologies greatly simplify constructing, editing, and sharing of documents, which may invite the creation of many low-quality products. But, suitably channeled, high-volume and high-speed production also has its good side. Obviously, the easier it is for individual faculty members to create courseware (or to tailor existing materials into new packages), the more they will be able to offer diverse materials to an expanding and increasingly divergent student population. Responding to a nearly overwhelming need for remedial instruction, for example, faculty from the California State University system might be able to put together a fresh physics curriculum in short order by combining some of the simpler digital simulations, assignments, and exams from any of the more than 25 physics courses now online in the World Lecture Hall.

This same flexibility could permit institutions to build new courseware and learning products that respond to the rapidly changing demands of industry—not, assuming popular predictions are right, a one-time effort. Former Labor Secretary Robert Reich, among others, claims that workers will need to retool for up to five job changes per career. If so, rapid changes in instructional materials will be the rule for the foreseeable future; and the versatility that new information technologies bring to educational production will be critical for meeting these demands.

In short, just as information technology already helps manufacturing and services industries to dramatically shorten production cycles and to help solve the challenge of just-in-time academic publishing, it could enable higher education to meet the demand for just-in-time or on-demand learning.

REFLECTION: MANY INTERESTING OPTIONS, MANY HARD CHOICES—A REPRISE

Viewed broadly, information technologies might change the ways instruction and learning materials are created much as they could alter the ways instruction and learning are delivered: by providing many different kinds of applications, not just one or a few. The applications could speak to a variety of goals and problems in higher education, helping to reduce costs, enrich and diversify course offerings, expand access, and increase responsiveness to industry demands and social needs; and some of the most valuable uses of information technology will not simply improve educational productivity, but will require institutions to consider moderate or extensive structural transformations.

For example, by digitizing library holdings, universities can expect to save space, reduce acquisition costs, seamlessly combine multimedia documents with traditional text, and provide students and faculty with a new generation of tools for finding information and organizing it into intellectual products. However, although a single university can benefit from digitization, cross-institutional cooperation may be critical if digital libraries are to make the best-quality materials available to students and to reach the broadest audience. As we have noted, copyright problems will challenge this kind of library merging, as will barriers between higher-education institutions.

By the same token, smaller, grassroots publishers on the Web, rather than larger, traditional publishing firms, look to be nimbler providers of new digital courseware that will meet changing industry needs. But, at least today, the individual publication process is chaotic, to say the least. In the World Lecture Hall, for instance, faculty often cut and paste new curricula from previous offerings, with little concern for copyright or institutional origin. This kind of highly informal cross-institutional collaboration has been common in academic research. Nevertheless, in the past, most higher-education institutions have been much more reluctant to share their course offerings, informally or otherwise. So, as with digital libraries, individual academic publishing may stress or even transform existing institutional structures, rather than simply enabling them to operate more productively without fundamental change.[4]

A slightly different way to view all this is that the Internet is beginning to foster new academic and learning communities across the Web, most of which are organizing along functional lines: developing courseware, conducting research, sharing curricula, for instance. Common interests and expertise are much more important in defining these communities than is distance, an impediment that cheap, high-bandwidth connectivity largely erases. For similar reasons, most cyberspace communities tend to ignore institutional boundaries when those boundaries interfere with emerging functional interests. These forces are beginning to give rise to new communities of practice that, at the very least, crisscross previous structures and may even erode old higher-education structures while building new ones. We discuss such communities in the next chapter.

---

[4]Or not. Perhaps the individual publishers will be transformed by existing institutional standards rather than change them. How freely authors will actually share their online curricula with others, for instance, remains an open question. Historically, the academic community, compared to for-profit publishers, has followed a very open policy. This may be changing. For example, increasingly, faculty are copyrighting their World Lecture Hall products; if enforced, these copyrights may have a chilling effect on cooperative courseware development. This and other intellectual property rights issues are discussed above in the section called Obstacles to Building Productive Digital Libraries.

Chapter Four

CREATING CONNECTED EDUCATIONAL COMMUNITIES

Chapters Two and Three consider how information technologies can contribute to two well-defined higher-education missions (delivering and creating instruction) and, in so doing, can address some major challenges that higher education now faces. But the preceding chapter discussed how the Internet, in particular, might play a much broader role: fostering electronic-learning communities. Not surprisingly, the potential effects of such communities on specific educational problems are much tougher to gauge than are those of more well-defined technologies, such as distance learning. For one thing, these communities often emerge spontaneously, rather than as part of a deliberate plan aimed at specific educational goals. Moreover, since Web-based groups are so new, it will be some time before we see which key problems in higher education they might help solve, if any. And, if online communities do help improve educational outcomes, almost certainly they will do so not simply by reducing labor costs and increasing the productivity of traditional higher-education-delivery systems, but by transforming learning and teaching practices.

In spite of these uncertainties, electronic-learning communities are worthy of attention, because, if they realize even a fraction of the benefits BioMedNet or the World Lecture Hall seem to promise, they will indeed make a substantial mark on higher education.

If you scan the WWW for online educational communities, it quickly becomes apparent that, however formative they may be, they are also ubiquitous. We have reviewed communities that conduct and publish research and share curricula; but others are appearing to fulfill almost every information-based function associated with higher-education institutions, both within and across traditional organizational boundaries. Within institutions, for example, governance and administration issues are being discussed not just through academic committee meetings but also using various network technologies, including e-mail, organized electronic discussion groups, real-time chat rooms, and Web pages. (See Figure 4.1.) Just as in other businesses, information technologies may cut out layers of academic middle management and give faculty more-direct input into institutional decisionmaking. This use of information technology to flatten organizational structure, which is hardly novel in business, is still rare in "cloistered" universities.

Internet applications such as these might help improve the flow of information within higher-education institutions and help accelerate internal decisionmaking. Perhaps the most interesting feature of most successful online communities, however, is that they often start small, with a single purpose (such as administration), then expand—not only attracting a larger collection of participants, but also adding functions. In this chapter, then, we briefly present a few such emerging communities, noting how they might address key challenges for higher education, but also keeping in mind how tentative these possibilities are, at least today. We first look at some of the vir-

> The University of California, Davis is using Web pages to help create a new Information Technology Strategic Plan (see http://it.ucdavis.edu/). The root page includes links to current versions of parts of the strategic plan, service guides and reference materials, University technology reports, as well as links that route browsers to any of UCD's current Information Technology Operating Units (e.g., The Center for Advanced Information Technology). All these links provide background material for faculty and Information Technology Strategic Planning Committee members, who can contribute to the ongoing planning and design process. Some of the planning was conducted in focus groups and face-to-face community meets. But later deliberations were conducted using online forums.

Figure 4.1—Academic Technology-Planning Using Information Technologies

tual communities that have been around the longest—those in academic publishing.

BIOMEDNET: AN EXAMPLE OF ELECTRONIC COMMUNITIES

BioMedNet (Figure 4.2) began its virtual life as a single electronic academic journal in 1991. Today, bolstered by the Web, which permits a richer collection of materials to be placed online (the early electronic journals relied mainly on text, and e-mail-like communication protocols), and an infusion of capital, BioMedNet has expanded its functionality to include an online library of publications, a shopping mall (which links to companies that sell products of interest to this community), a collection of collaboration tools, and even an electronic bulletin board of job opportunities. (See Figure 4.2.) Virtual discussion groups and online conferences are the most recent additions to this growing community.

BioMedNet and many of its contemporaries look at once familiar and novel. The individual services they provide all have analogs in traditional academic communities: Libraries permit faculty and students to take out books on loan, meeting rooms are available for conferences, administration offices can arrange purchases on individual or institutional accounts, and department bulletin boards post flyers that announce new academic positions. However, several features may make the online versions more powerful than their analogs.

One feature is that the pieces of and participants in these online communities can be seamlessly combined. BioMedNet offers higher-education faculty in biological and medical science almost "one-stop shopping" for professional needs: In a couple of hours, professors might be able to catch up on the latest journal publications, read critical reviews, discuss new research ideas with colleagues from other countries, examine new books in their field, check out job listings, and place orders for a variety of products. These examples certainly do not exhaust the online services these providers will soon offer (and which the growing communities will soon demand). One recent addition in BioMedNet, for instance, permits members to create their own virtual rooms within the community. These rooms can contain a profile (which helps BioMedNet

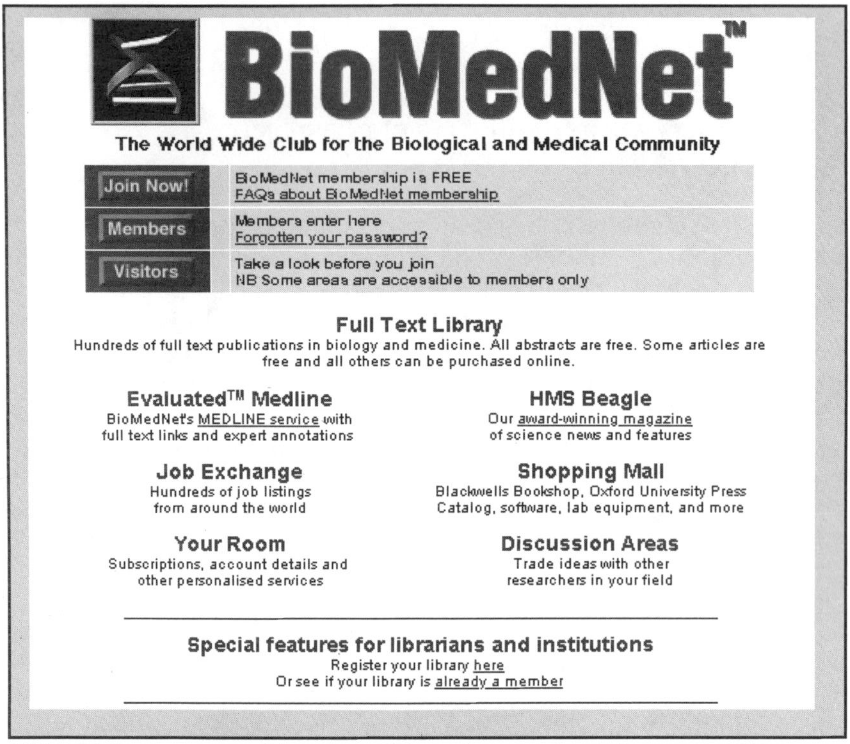

SOURCE: Image excerpted from http://biomednet.com/ on February 26, 1998.

Figure 4.2—BioMedNet Homepage

suggest products and people of interest), details of their credit-card accounts (to facilitate electronic purchases), monthly billing statements (with a complete record of past purchases), and a community e-mail account (for corresponding with BioMedNet members only, not the Internet at large).

If designed properly, some virtual parts of electronic communities may actually do much more than their paper counterparts do, not simply provide the same services more conveniently. For example, job listings do not need to be (and in some Web sites are not) limited to static announcements of required qualifications and pay ranges. Links can permit Web applicants to visit homepages of potential employers, or even to take online tests and interviews. They can draw into a growing community a wide range of educational stakeholders who rarely talk to one another. As the environment sketched in Figure 4.3 suggests, information technologies already provide, for

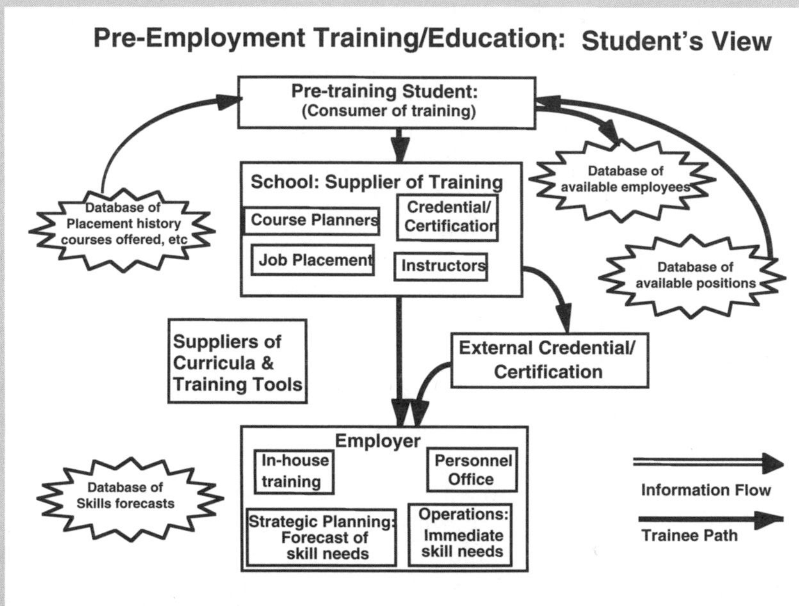

This information environment was designed as part of a RAND transition-to-work study. One of the main goals of the research was to provide models for how network technologies could help increase the bandwidth and flexibility of communication among students, schools, and the workplace. Implemented as Web homepages, the prototype system connected a local vocational school, and its students, to nearby employers. As part of the work, the project also showed how several kinds of databases, describing schools, students, skills, and jobs, could be constructed to add substantial value to the network as a whole.

Figure 4.3—A Schematic of a Possible Information Environment to Support the Transition to Work

example, tools that help students learn about employment opportunities, let employers converse with candidate workers, and enable schools to keep up-to-date about the changing needs of the job market. And the more these networked communities extend to new participants and link them in different ways, the more new communication technologies appear to be redefining the educational communities, rather then just streamlining communities that already exist.

It is a good bet that more-expansive communities—communities that fulfill even more-innovative functions and encompass a broader collection of stakeholders than existing communities, such as BioMedNet—will appear shortly. At present, however, the best, or at least the most complete, of these electronic communities seem focused on research and academic publication rather than on other missions of higher education. This focus may be beginning to change, as some institutions start to take the idea of combining educational functions in electronic communities to its logical conclusion: the virtual university.

VIRTUAL UNIVERSITIES: OLD WINE IN NEW BOTTLES?

While the realization of an entire virtual university seems the inevitable end-state of a movement to digitize higher education, many institutions have been "virtualizing" themselves, in bits and pieces, for years. Recall that the Open University (Chapter Two), probably still the world's largest "virtual campus" (however this loose term is defined), has been using telecommunications to offer distance learning for over three decades. In the past, OU and others relied mainly on TV, radio, and telephony; today, the Internet and WWW are the vehicles of choice as universities go online. According to the Institute for Learning Technologies at Columbia University (http://daemon.ilt.columbia.edu/ilt/), almost 500 universities in the United States already have some Web presence, which, in many cases, still means just a homepage providing a brief description of the institution, its mission, and addresses to contact if the Internet browser wants any real information about admissions, requirements, or courses. The next steps beyond basic public relations often include virtual campus tours using interactive maps, digital campus periodicals or newspapers, homepages for specific departments, university centers and faculty, and online application forms.

These sites provide prospective students with a wealth of information they can use in planning their college careers. As of winter 1996, however, only a few established public or private universities had "virtualized" core teaching and learning functions.[1] And, of those that had, most still limit online offerings in several ways:

- The University of British Columbia provides online courses that are mainly *about* the Internet itself, rather than about other subjects.
- UWired (part of the University of Washington) also weights its offerings toward net courses, and also follows the strategy of overlaying networked courseware on existing courses—the online resources are essentially enrichment materials—rather than creating stand-alone virtual courses.
- Arcadia University boasts an attractive set of pages at its Web site, but it offers only continuing education classes at a distance (using video rather than the Internet).

Perhaps not surprisingly, the most complete virtual universities on the Internet are not extensions of existing institutions but institutions that have been created in cyberspace almost from scratch.

Athena

By no means rivaling their traditional counterparts in size of faculty or range of courses, online universities such as Athena (Figure 4.4) are beginning to put together digital versions of all the familiar pieces of a campus. Founded in 1995, Athena had, by April 1996, employed about 25 faculty (some full-time and others who teach at traditional universities) and offered courses in over a dozen subject areas. Like a typical university, Athena grants liberal arts degrees (although it is

---

[1]This statement demands further research. At a minimum, the following questions should be addressed: How many universities are doing more than public relations on the Web? What kinds of services are they providing online? Who are they and what are their strategies (existing institutions, virtualizing bit-by-bit, or new virtual campuses created from scratch)? Answering these questions definitively, though, is like hitting a moving target: The number of universities online changes daily. For instance, Peterson's (1997) *Distance Learning Programs,* New York, Peterson's Guides, Inc., counted 97 "cyberschools" in 1993; in 1997 this total was almost 800.

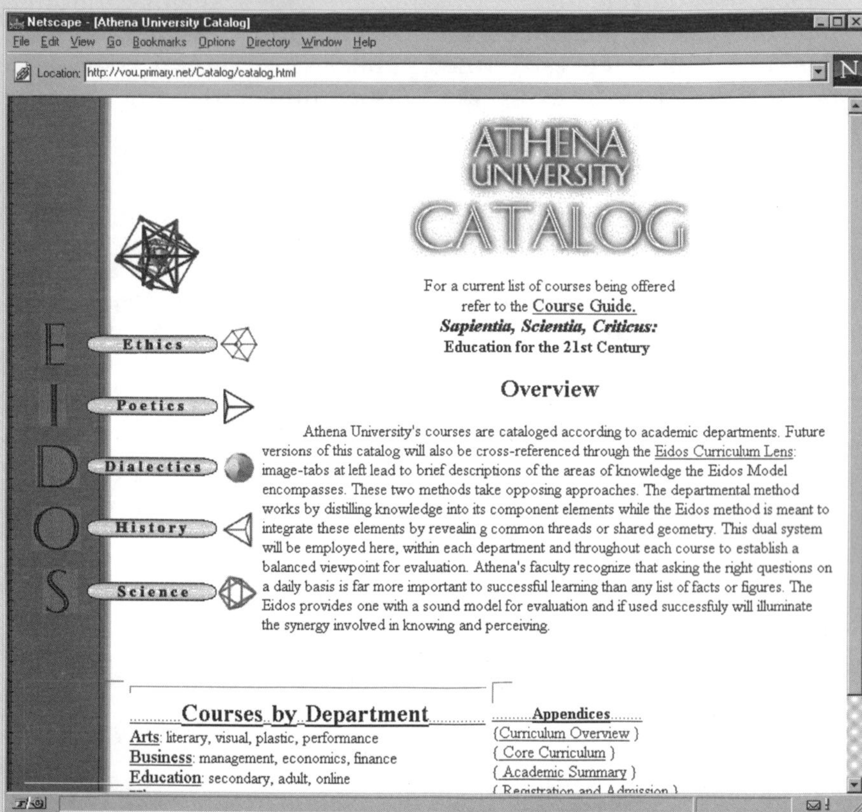

This is Athena's course catalog, which provides links to specific course descriptions, as well as to admission requirements, registration information, degree requirements, and the core curriculum. In addition, users can quickly link to an online student guide and faculty directory. The student guide provides detailed instructions on how to use the online technology that makes up Athena's infrastructure. The faculty directory lists all current staff and provides e-mail links to most, and homepages and vitae for many.

Athena is administered by Virtual Online University, Inc., a nonprofit corporation offering a novel approach to academic excellence, professional development, and life-long learning.

SOURCE: Image excerpted from http://vou.primary.net/Catalog/catalog.html on February 27, 1998.

Figure 4.4—Athena University: A Familiar Organization in a New Medium?

still waiting to receive accreditation from a regional accreditation body), has a transfer-credit policy, and offers a detailed, and surprisingly traditional, core curriculum. Athena differs substantially from most higher-education institutions only in its admission policy (because finite resources such as classroom space are not an issue, enrollment is open and unlimited) and its teaching methods.

Like courses in the World Lecture Hall, all Athena courses rely heavily on the Web. However, Athena courses go beyond typical WWW homepages, which are often rich multimedia documents, but rarely documents that permit the kind of intensive interaction among students and teachers that are the hallmark of good learning environments. Following others who seek to develop high-quality learning environments for the Web (Figure 2.9), Athena's idea is to mix the richness of Web documents with the dialogue of MOOs (multi-user, object-oriented environments), which introduce into the WWW world of graphics, audio, and text, a communication protocol that permits students and teachers to talk with one another across the network in real-time, and to share multimedia "objects" as they chat.

Athena is a conscious attempt to capture the best of a traditional university structure in a virtual version. If it acquires accreditation and can keep costs low while continuing to offer courses to all comers, Athena could succeed in this goal.[2] But Athena's is not the only approach to developing a virtual university, nor is it necessarily the best one. A few groups are viewing cyberspace as an opportunity to rethink the structure of educational institutions from the foundations up, rather than as a new tool for an existing organization. The Globewide Network Academy (GNA) is an example of such a rethought institution.

GNA

The Globewide Network Academy (http://www.gnacademy.org) is one such experiment. (See Figure 4.5.) In a broad sense, GNA is a

---

[2]As of winter 1996, however, a liberal arts degree from Athena did not come cheap at approximately $12,000 (120 credit hours at $100 per hour). Costs may drop in the future if Athena can attract more students while requiring relatively few added faculty. But, even now, Athena clearly undercuts higher-education institutions (where degrees usually cost over $25,000) and private schools (where $50,000 is rarely enough).

This is from an online letter by the president of GNA, July 1995:

What is the Globewide Network Academy?

The Globewide Network Academy is a federation of educational and research institutions. We exist in order to provide a central location at which students and teachers can find each other, and to provide administrative support services to aid teachers in teaching.

Much of the reason for the existence of GNA lies in the belief that the traditional departmental structure of universities is reaching the end of its usefulness and that new organizational structures are needed if universities are to provide education for the masses of the world with the diminishing resources which are available to them.

Universities today are both too large and too small. An average university is simply too large to have a coherent focus, and most universities today are indeed composed of many sub-groups many of whom have conflicting ideas of where the university should go. As a result, one has huge amounts of energy being wasted in academic politics when in becomes necessary for the university to set priorities.

At the same time universities are too small. If you go to five different universities, you generally find five different registrar departments, five different payroll departments, five different computational systems, etc. etc. This leads to tremendous and costly administrative duplication which serves absolutely no educational purpose.

At the same time, universities are facing increasing pressures from the outside. Tuitions are rising far beyond the ability of a middle class family to pay, and government grants for research and education are drying up as governments face budgetary pressures. At the same time, universities are victims of their own success as the doctoral students that they are producing are unable to find any job openings in traditional academia.

The purpose behind the federation model of GNA is to deal with both of the structural problems of the traditional university so that it can deal with the challenges that face it in the opening years of the 21st century. GNA consists of independent members, each of whom has their own internal finances and course and curriculum policies. The core organization is responsible for providing computational and administrative support as well as providing a central location for students to find the courses that they are looking for.

SOURCE: Excerpted from http://www.gnacademy.org:8001/HyperNews/get/ documents/pres-letter.html on February 27, 1998.

Figure 4.5—Globewide Network Academy: A New Organization in a New Medium?

mix of Athena and the World Lecture Hall. Like Athena (and unlike the World Lecture Hall), GNA offers more than a collection of online courses; it also includes virtual lounges where teachers, students, administrative and support staff, and technical experts can engage in ongoing electronic discussions about the academy. The student lounge also contains a collection of links that make up an ad hoc digital library and another set of links to career resources.

Like the World Lecture Hall (and unlike Athena), GNA is not developing its own courses. Rather, it encourages institutions and individuals to list with GNA existing courses for online distance learning, then provides a collection of value-adding and brokering services to help students find the courseware they want and to put them in contact with the providing institutions. At the same time, GNA offers support services for teachers and contributing institutions, which, they hope, will improve the quantity and quality of the products GNA manages. Initial indications look promising: By 1996, GNA had already catalogued thousands of courses, contributed by almost 200 sponsoring members (mostly American public universities—including Athena).

REFLECTION: NETWORKED COMMUNITIES AND HIGHER-EDUCATION GOALS

Electronic communities now emerging on the Internet and WWW may address several key goals of and challenges for higher education. In the simplest cases, putting basic functions online will streamline existing communication processes, helping both to reduce costs and increase access. Enrolling through the Web, or e-mail, already saves paperwork and administrative time; students also avoid long lines and frustrating delays in finding courses with open spots that suit their needs. But, although valuable, these uses of information technology with the Internet are certainly not new.

New network communities are just beginning to take advantage of the unique characteristics of the Internet and Web to fulfill a wide range of educational functions. Within higher-education institutions, Web-based dialogues might help open up decision-making processes and flatten administrative structure. If lessons from the corporate use of information technologies hold here, universities might be encouraged to rethink more rapidly the products (courses) they offer, thereby being more responsive to the needs of business. Such responsiveness might be enhanced further if the same networks that improve communication within higher education also provide direct links to the business community, giving students direct access to potential employers, enabling employers to query schools for lists of promising prospective workers, and permitting industry more of a say in academic course design.

As electronic communities continue to grow, they should help meet more of higher education's pressing needs. But growth means more than expanding to include a larger number of students and faculty; it also means connecting a broader set of stakeholders and encompassing additional educational functions. Such growth seems to point to virtual universities as a kind of holy grail for higher education: a single cyber-institution that provides all the functions of the academy, digitized and knit tightly together through high-bandwidth network connections. Certainly, virtual universities look like the logical conclusion of all this digital construction in that it is hard to imagine a digital academy that is more inclusive in its functions. Athena and others are deliberately attempting to build cyber-institutions that include as many pieces as possible of existing universities, from student centers, to libraries, to classrooms and faculty lounges. Some even include images of virtual ivy-covered walls. That these visions are so all-encompassing and vivid is, perhaps, the main reason that the popular press seem to view virtual universities as the most cutting-edge and ambitious of all applications of information technology to higher education.

Ambitious? Yes. Cutting-edge? Not really. Certainly, building anything that has the scope of a fully virtual university is challenging to say the least. But although the technology is thoroughly modern, the institutions being constructed in Athena, and those planned by other developers, are actually about as traditional as can be. GNA, on the other hand, demonstrates that a virtual university might *transform the structure* of higher education rather than simply streamlining it or improving its productivity (in any simple sense). GNA is trying to do more than digitize the past: while it replicates some conventional functions (e.g., virtual student lounges), a few familiar functions are distributed or eliminated (e.g., databases collect courses from other higher-education institutions; GNA does not create them), and still others seem quite new (e.g., GNA's brokering services to connect providers with consumers).

None of this suggests that GNA is more likely to succeed as a virtual university than Athena. Both may succeed or fail. And, in any case, their fates may have little to do with their underlying structures.

The comparison is important in that it illuminates two broader points. First, network-based information technologies can be used to deliver educational services in many different ways. Athena and GNA are two options, but doubtless others soon will surface that are more radical than GNA in the way they reorganize traditional functions of higher education—partnering with more-global institutions for digital library services or offering education on a "per-concept" basis, rather than providing whole programs of study, for instance. With equal certainty, other virtual universities will appear on the Web that are as traditional as Athena. It is in the nature of a flexible new technology such as the Web that it can be as easily configured to mimic an existing institutional structure or medium (Figure 1.1) as it can be crafted into a novel structure. If anything, repeating the past with new technology is easier than devising new designs, which takes considerable creativity, and substantial hard testing and refining to prove.

This brings up the second point. Many public and private higher-education institutions have been reluctant to experiment with novel applications of information technology, not only because they are tougher to devise and more expensive to implement, but because digitizing old institutions may still seem like a perfectly serviceable, and much more certain, strategy. However, if current higher-education institutions are not interested in conducting high-risk experiments, new external providers of educational services are. If they succeed, they may make holding to the status quo less and less tenable.

Chapter Five

COMPETING WITH NEW EXTERNAL PROVIDERS OF EDUCATION

Higher-education institutions may be skittish about the uncertainties associated with innovative uses of information technology to build learning communities. But a growing collection of external providers—mainly proprietary, for-profit institutions—are embracing them. A brief review of these external providers can yield several insights for higher education, allowing them to size up the competition, suggesting some concrete models of technology-based reforms worth borrowing, and even offering opportunities for collaboration as well as strategies for competition. Because the literature on these new providers is scant, we limit ourselves to discussing just a few examples.[1]

WHAT ARE EXTERNAL PROVIDERS?

The proprietary training sector covers a wide range of schools and providers. Some grant degrees; others offer only short courses and

[1]Surveying external providers would be a worthy research topic. Many basic questions beg answers:

- How many of these online external providers are offering contract training?
- How many are now shifting over to offering "serious" higher-education courses?
- How are growing demands for "knowledge workers" affecting the demand for these providers?
- What will new business practices that rely on them look like (presumably decentralized, networked, transformed by information technology itself)?

An understanding of external providers would give higher education a better foundation for thinking about how to train knowledge workers and, therefore, how to compete (or partner) with new providers that are already training them.

training seminars. Some focus on routine clerical, sales, and cosmetics skills; still others offer professional classes in law and architecture. About the only feature all share is that fees and tuition cover costs, since none is supported directly through taxes. Because their operations are so different, it has been difficult to measure the size of this sector in relation to public and private academic institutions. Clearly, however, it is a large and growing sector. California alone now boasts thousands of proprietary schools (compared with 200 or so traditional higher-education institutions), bringing in an estimated $1.4 billion in tuition as of 1992. This sector promises to expand substantially because, in the future, businesses (not individuals) will be the primary clients. In 1994, businesses spent roughly $50 billion on training. Whereas much of that training was done in-house in the past, it is increasingly being outsourced to external providers.

Probably the biggest, and certainly the fastest-expanding, part of this sector belongs to companies providing training in using new information technologies. In 1995, corporations in the United States paid over $15 billion in information-technology training, a figure that will probably grow about 15 percent per year to over $30 billion by the end of the century. Such courses cover everything from mastering the nuances of Windows 95 to acquiring much more generic skills in object-oriented programming, analysis, and design. Not surprisingly, the courses are not only about high technology but *use* that technology, originating, generally, with external providers who specialize in training products that make the heaviest, and often most innovative, uses of information technology. Some, such as The Teaching Company (Figure 2.10) and Learning Tree (http://www.lrntree.com/) offer thousands of computer-based training (CBT) course products, most created to meet the needs of large corporate clients. Microsoft, Intel, Novell, and other large software and hardware companies also offer a wide range of training courses. But theirs are courses tailored primarily to their own products, rather than to clients' interests.

MICROSOFT TAKES OVER

At first glance, Microsoft's OnLine Institute (MOLI) at http://moli.microsoft.com/[2] resembles Athena in several ways. In some respects aiming at one-stop shopping for training, it supplies online enrollment, certification programs, exam preparation, and a list of Web-based courses. (See Figure 5.1.) But MOLI's relationship with students, course providers, and specific classes is actually anything but traditional. More like GNA than Athena, MOLI mainly furnishes the infrastructure and value-added services that organize Web-based courses on such products as Visual Basic, C++, and Word. Third-party online content vendors (OCVs) develop most of the interactive courseware products; different groups, called authorized online classroom providers (OCPs), build specific classes from these materials, adding human learning advisors and other curriculum material as needed. Students then interact with MOLI by searching the course-list database to find OCPs whose courses meet their needs and whose location is suitable. (Distance matters for a subset of the courses that include extensive face-to-face interaction with learning advisors.) Students also can make use of various common information resources in MOLI, such as the student union, library, advising center, and bookstore.

Just as it provides various tools to help consumers, MOLI also attends very carefully to its suppliers. In contrast to the World Lecture Hall, which seems to accept all course offerings it receives, MOLI constrains course providers in at least three ways. First, the Institute defines the topics (the Microsoft products and programming skills) for which it will accept courseware. Second, it evaluates courseware and classes, and admits only those OCVs and OCPs that it authorizes.

---

[2]As of October 1997, MOLI no longer resides at this location; Figure 5.1 is also obsolete. We have retained the following discussion, however, because the contents, products, and services of MOLI have not been abandoned by Microsoft. Rather, MOLI has been integrated into Microsoft's Authorized Technical Education Center (see http://www.microsoft.com/atec), which combines both Web-based training and traditional classroom instruction in one site. The disappearance of MOLI, therefore, is not a testament to the short life-span of many digital ventures. On the contrary, it underscores how readily Web-based services can be combined or transformed into new—and presumably better—ones.

Third, it imposes standards for courseware development that help ensure that Web-based content developed by different OCVs will run on a wide range of platforms and will work well when put together into larger course products. MOLI encourages content vendors and course providers to meet these demands by offering tools and infrastructure, including the bookstore and library, that help create high-quality products. But the primary incentive is financial: OCVs can sell curricula to OCPs and to other interested (but not authorized) parties through the MOLI bookstore; OCPs sell courseware directly to individual students or corporate clients.

This model for instruction delivery has many interesting features, some also shared by communities such as Athena and GNA, but oth-

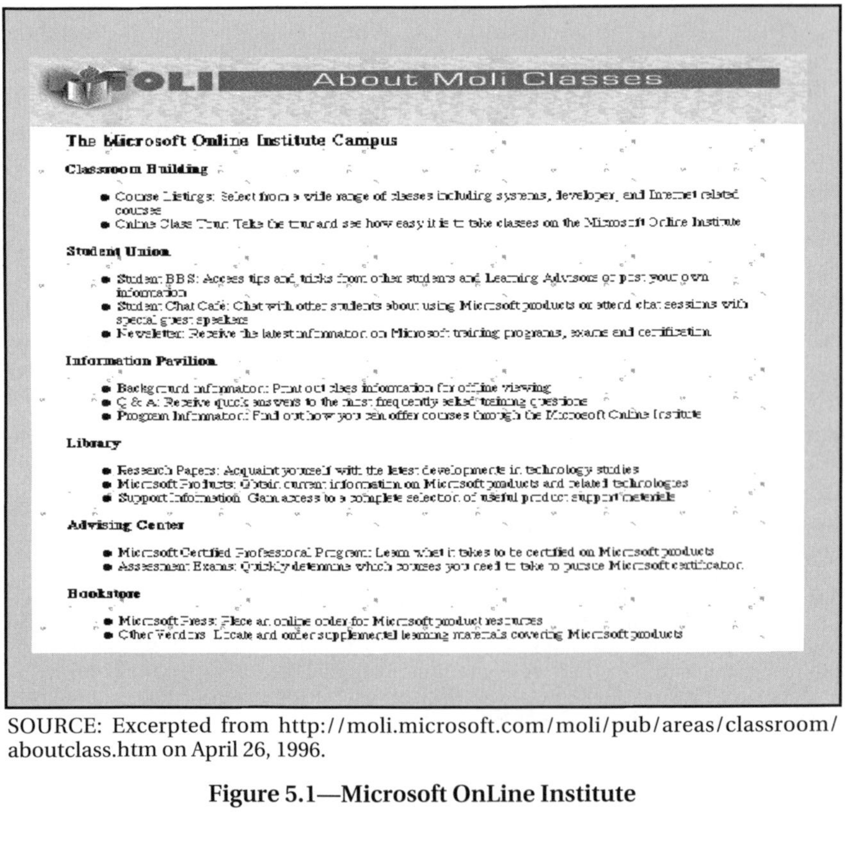

SOURCE: Excerpted from http://moli.microsoft.com/moli/pub/areas/classroom/aboutclass.htm on April 26, 1996.

Figure 5.1—Microsoft OnLine Institute

ers that look quite new. Because MOLI has no physical infrastructure and few labor expenses, the cost of courses is low. (It is not clear that Microsoft makes a penny from MOLI, since its main goal is to sell software, not training.) By carefully managing its third-party vendors, MOLI can effectively provide just-in-time training services; vendors move rapidly to create courses for new Microsoft products, to reach the market ahead of their many competitors. Also, like Athena and GNA, Microsoft is concerned with assessment exams and certification of students. However, in contrast to other virtual universities, MOLI has no concept of admission or courseload; students simply purchase instruction as needed (or as required by their employers), course by course, if not concept by concept.

TRAINING MODEL VERSUS HIGHER-EDUCATION MODEL

All this might seem right for corporate training, but what lessons might higher education draw from such a model? On the surface, training is a very different sector from higher education. Most training skills are relatively narrow and well-defined, whereas skills taught in higher education are usually broader in scope and more difficult to quantify. Business skills also typically turn over more rapidly than those targeted by higher education. Microsoft needs new courses every year for the many software products it creates, buys, or modifies; university classes often stay relatively fixed, in part because the topics they address—intellectual and cultural artifacts, from philosophy to algebra—change slowly, if at all. The sectors also differ in the wealth of the clients they serve, as well as in the nature of the skills they target. Businesses routinely spend much more per worker on training than public education spends per student. Training providers can use this high profit margin to invest in new training technology, while higher-education institutions often find the price tag for new information technology too high.

However, these differences are diminishing; indeed, previously distinct boundaries between the higher-education and corporate-training markets may be beginning to blur. For one thing, higher-education institutions are coming under pressure to change their course offerings more quickly and to make them responsive to the demands of business. The resulting curricula often focus more on applied knowledge than do the ones they are supplanting. Corporate training is also moving in this direction, although from a very different starting point. In the past, most training schemes were vocational (helping mechanics fine-tune skills on new machines, for example); today, more and more cater to knowledge workers in their never-ending quest for life-long learning. Creative thinking and higher-order problem solving, topics once the exclusive domain of higher education, are slowly crowding out learning of routine procedures in training courses. Even now it is hard to distinguish, say, a computer-aided drafting course at a proprietary school from one offered by a community college or a university.

At the same time, although today it is still easier to create courseware for training classes on programming and using spreadsheets, information technologies are becoming increasingly useful in education classes that focus on more-complex (and less-well-defined) problem-solving skills, as many of the Internet and Web tools we reviewed already attest. Further, as these technologies continue to drop in price, higher education should become an increasingly profitable market for them.

In short, education and training are merging in two senses: just as the content of training is becoming more like the content of higher-education classes, the feasibility and profitability of technology-based courses for higher education are rising to the level of computer-based training.

REFLECTION: HIGHER EDUCATION, EXTERNAL PROVIDERS, AND INFORMATION TECHNOLOGY—FLIGHT, FIGHT, OR FRIENDS?

How, then, does information technology affect higher education's challenges of competing with new external providers? If anything, it is exacerbating, not easing, them. Several strands of evidence argue that proprietary providers already think that information technology has helped reduce delivery costs to the point where even "down-market" (read: higher-education) services can be delivered profitably. A growing number of companies now straddle both sectors, in many cases offering essentially the same courseware products to each. Academic Systems (http://www.academic.com/), for example, has had banner years in both sectors. Just after receiving $12 million from Microsoft, TCI, and Accel Partners to develop corporate training programs that can be dialed up on a user's home computer, Academic Systems got high marks for its CD-ROM–based algebra curricula in California State University classrooms.

This is just one example of what will probably be an important trend in the coming decade. Several niches in what may eventually be a vast market in adult learning are apparently ripe for technology-based educational services. For-profit companies are tapping each of them aggressively. Academic Systems is marketing directly to higher-education institutions. Others, such as The Teaching Company, look primarily to the home market. Many of them also offer educational software to corporate clients, for remedial instruction. Whereas, in the past, corporate training has focused mainly on job-specific skills,[3] businesses now also are under increasing pressure to provide remedial instruction for employees (for learning that probably should have been acquired in college or even high school, but was not). In different guises, all these growing areas are calling for roughly the kinds of learning that higher education typically has offered. But, except in traditional higher-education markets (young adults coming straight out of high school), universities and colleges are largely ceding these opportunities to proprietary providers.

Flight

Higher-education institutions as a whole have not formulated plans to deal with the increasing encroachment of external providers on their "turf." They need to. These providers enjoy several advantages over higher education that enable them to devise creative systems for delivering training and education on the Internet and Web. To begin with, many are technically savvy and heavily capitalized. (Today, for example, Microsoft probably invests more in educational-technology R&D than the federal government does.) This means that external education providers often have both the financial and intellectual assets they need to experiment with high-risk/high-gain educational designs. Perhaps more important, when designing schools or other

[3]Companies are naturally reluctant to pay employees to acquire broadly valuable skills, since these skills will make them more attractive to other firms too, not just more valuable to the employer.

delivery systems for learning, external providers have the great luxury of starting with a clean slate: no need, for instance, to assume that classes will meet at a set time, to worry about faculty displaced by software, nor to fight with teachers' unions. Consequently, when external providers craft their designs, they can focus on what the technology makes possible and what services their clients demand, rather than worrying about how to shoe-horn new designs into existing educational structures.

At the very least, then, these providers offer innovative models for using information technology that higher education should attend to. But, after learning from them, what actions to take?

Fight

One approach is to shore up defenses against invaders into traditional higher-education markets, for example, by erecting protectionist barriers that discourage new providers from entering the battle. Some would argue that the tax supports that public institutions now enjoy do just that. Perhaps a more positive tactic is to improve productivity in the face of new competition. Many of the enterprises we have reviewed—distance-learning campuses and virtual universities, for example—can be regarded as ways in which higher education already is trying to become more productive, sometimes by borrowing models of delivery from the training sector, and often by creating innovative models of its own.

A different strategy is to take the offensive, rather than honing defenses. Inspired in part by movements of external providers into higher education's turf, a few institutions are beginning to respond to the challenges posed by external providers by moving, however cautiously, into contract training. Of all higher-education institutions, the community colleges have shown by far the most initiative here. (See Figure 5.2.) A few years ago, about half of all community colleges did some contract training with business; today, about 90 percent do. Some community-college experts even see training as the solution to their financial problems and expect that contract training will become the biggest piece of the community-college system.

Still, higher education faces several imposing difficulties in this migration, some of them technical. Corporations, for example, expect personalized, on-site training services; external providers increasingly deliver these tailored courses through wired or even satellite-based network technologies. Community colleges will need comparable tools in order to offer quality courseware at a competitive per-person price that is equally responsive to clients' needs.

Other challenges are organizational, reflecting the fact that community colleges (unlike external providers) do not have carte blanche for building their contract training services. Business clients, for example, frequently expect to be able to mix their instructors with college personnel; however, doing so often conflicts with union contracts that forbid colleges to hire external staff. Also, some contracting arrangements threaten informal or formal community-college rules requiring that the college serve mainly local needs (tough to adhere to if contract training is shipped across the state via networks) or demanding that classes be open to all students (senseless if courseware is designed for specific corporate clients).

CORPORATE TRAINING

Although community colleges have been in the corporate training marketplace for some time, they now are reaching out more aggressively, and the American Association of Community Colleges says that about 90% of its member colleges are involved to some extent in the business of training workers for specific companies, rather than just teaching generic subjects or trades. Cost-conscious community colleges have a natural advantage competing for this business against four-year institutions, which may be too proud, too well-off, or too bureaucratic to show much real interest in the training needs of the local business community. A key indicator of successful community college corporate programs is the college's willingness to bring instruction to the client's workplace, rather than requiring students to come to its campus. (David Stamps, "Community Colleges Go Corporate," *Training*, December 1995, p. 36)

SOURCE: Edupage, January 16, 1996.

Figure 5.2—Higher Education Invades Corporate Training

Friends

While community colleges struggle to compete with external providers in the contract-training market, other higher-education institutions are starting to evolve different strategies, some involving cooperative partnerships as much as competition. In this battle, the size of long-established universities, while often a liability in times that demand nimble change, actually can work to their advantage. For one thing, some training needs are so vast that they attract only the largest providers.

For example, in 1996, Michigan announced a large-scale educational program that would use the Web to deliver a wide range of courses. (See Figure 5.3; also see http://www.mvac.org/.) Centered around the Virtual Michigan Auto College (Auto U), the idea is to help train the next generation of auto-industry workers, and thus to keep the industry firmly centered in Michigan. This is far too big a training job for any proprietary training school to manage by itself, so the plan is to build Auto U as a collection of state schools, led by the University of Michigan and all tied together through the Web.

Auto U looks innovative from several perspectives. First, many courses will be designed by teams drawn from Auto U and business

MICHIGAN FOCUSES ON THE AUTO JOBS OF THE FUTURE

DETROIT, Feb 28.—The Governor or Michigan today called for a large-scale education program that would use computer networks and tax credits to help train workers for future job openings in the automobile industry. . . .

The Governor said that to boost skills the state would create a virtual university called Auto U, consisting of courses taught on the Internet. Students could use computers to take classes focusing on the auto industry.

In addition, [Governor] Engler said the state would act as a sort of employment agency for the auto industry. The Michigan Employment Security Commission will use applications – in person and over the Internet—to screen job seekers.

SOURCE: *The Wall Street Journal,* February 28, 1996.

Figure 5.3—Auto U

partners, giving business a much stronger voice in curriculum planning than it usually enjoys. Second, the Internet apparently will play multiple roles here, beyond connecting students with instruction and linking businesses into course design. Using Web sites connected to Auto U, the state's employment commission will provide instant access to all Michigan online automotive information for students and prospective employees. Students will even be able to take virtual occupation tours, learning directly from workers about the types of jobs available in plants today and the skills needed to do them. (See also Figure 4.3.)

In short, Auto U appears to have the key trait of healthy electronic-learning communities, beginning with one or two core functions, then quickly adding new functions and new stakeholder groups. The third innovative feature of Auto U is the addition of one such group: As well as public higher-education institutions, the Auto U partnership will also include some for-profit trainers. As such, it may be one of the first examples of a cooperative arrangement that includes higher education, external training providers, and business.

Since Auto U is still barely off the drawing board, it is too early to tell how this cooperative partnership between higher education and external providers will work. Several relationships are possible. Perhaps reminiscent of Athena, principal partners (the University of Michigan) might retain considerable control, contracting out specific courses or services to specialized providers; more like MOLI, the higher-education partners could manage, set goals, and ensure courseware quality while delegating much courseware development to external partners; even less constrained relationships, as exemplified by GNA, might work.

However, one common feature in all these possibilities is the role that the Internet and Web will play in tying together the different partners in this evolving community. As we have seen, networks permit courseware and design discussions (as well as instruction delivery) to be shared readily, both within institutions and across their boundaries, enabling a collection of very different (and physically remote) institutions jointly to construct new educational curricula. Absent rich network connections, such heterogeneous models of education and training delivery simply were not feasible in the past. But, if Michigan can make this experiment work, these models may become increasingly popular in the future.

Chapter Six

ADDRESSING PLANNING AND POLICY: HOW TO MAKE THE BEST USE OF THE INTERNET AND WWW IN HIGHER EDUCATION

Anyone who began reading this report with the expectation that simple prescriptions would be given for increasing productivity in higher education using information technology might be confused at this point, if not disappointed. Far from sketching an easy fix, we have reviewed a wide array of Internet and Web-based applications for education and training. And the applications are not just numerous; they differ along many dimensions:

- Distance-learning systems aim (at least primarily) to increase access to learning while reducing costs.
- Cutting-edge applications, such as intelligent tutoring systems and simulation-based trainers, increase the quality of learning but will not help institutions deal with shrinking budgets (at least in the short term).
- Individual publishing may be the best way to provide a new generation of learning materials that are responsive to consumer and business needs (although this approach is much newer and less certain than traditional publishing).
- Online communities might help in meeting many challenges in higher education (yet most seem to operate outside current institutional structures rather than within them).
- External providers of training and educational services are making some of the most innovative uses of the Internet (but it is rarely clear how higher education should use these models and whether to do so in new markets, such as contract training, or in more-traditional venues).

In this chapter, we first look at what really works in information technology as applied to education, an area that is complicated at best. We then offer specific recommendations about how higher education should think about the Internet and WWW in its future planning.

REALITY CHECK: WHAT REALLY WORKS NOW AND WHAT WILL WORK IN THE FUTURE

We have reviewed many applications of information technology and the Internet in higher education, and many look enticing. But before beginning what might be an extensive and costly reorganization to accommodate them in classrooms, universities would, naturally, like some assurance that these new tools can really deliver what they appear to promise.

How solid is the evidence that the various Internet and Web technologies can really address important goals and problems in higher education? Not very. Without question, some educational tools have been evaluated very carefully. (See Figure 2.1 for examples.) Many distance-learning programs in higher education, for example, have demonstrated that the cost of delivering courses can be reduced substantially while keeping student outcomes approximately constant. A few "augmented" distance-learning programs have also improved student learning. For instance, at Stanford University, students learning physics through Tutored Video Instruction (whereby students watch videotaped lectures, replaying them off-campus, using a small-group, cooperative-learning format) outperformed students who actually attended lectures. Similarly, at both high-school and college levels, some of the best intelligent-tutoring systems have fulfilled their goal of increasing the quality of student learning. Algebra, geometry, and computer-programming tutoring systems developed at Carnegie-Mellon University, to take one of the most well-known successes, can raise scores on exams up to one full letter grade. On a broader scale, meta-analyses—which aggregate results of many separate experimental studies—show a smaller, but still statistically significant, effect of computer-based education.

What Works in Business

In many ways, the data for corporate training are both simpler and more compelling than those for education. Most companies want to train employees to become competent in relatively well-defined skills (using word processors, spreadsheets, or more specialized tools and software, for instance). Improvements in proficiency in these skills can be easily measured. By the same token, it is easy to gauge how much is saved by delivering this training through video rather than using in-person instructors, as are the additional gains in flexibility and further cost reduction achieved by moving from conventional video to Web-based TV delivery systems. For many corporations, the results are impressive enough to justify investing billions of dollars each year in technology-based training.

But these clear successes of information technology in education and training are limited in many ways. First, as the examples from corporate training suggest, most of the solid evidence concerns a few very well-defined skills. Standard tests can reliably measure how accurately a spreadsheet is used, how fast an algebra problem is solved, and even how well a software routine is written. However, although these are valuable talents, they only scratch the surface of the kinds of abilities we want higher education, if not corporate training, to foster. Complex skills—some specific to particular subjects, and others more generic, such as collaborative problem solving—are difficult to measure; therefore, it is difficult to show that information technologies improve how they are learned. But then, for these skills, it is currently impossible to demonstrate that *any* method of instruction delivery, whether it exploits the Internet or not, leads to improved learning. If this limitation disproportionately affects tools for learning and teaching that make heavy use of information technology, such as the Internet or Web, it is because they are often strongly associated with curriculum reforms that advocate teaching new, probably valuable but certainly ill-defined, kinds of knowledge.

A more straightforward reason for the scarcity of data demonstrating the value of Internet-based learning is that these applications are very new. While earlier generations of distance learning have acquired a certain pedigree with time, distance-learning courses that rely on high-bandwidth networks are now at most a few years old—barely enough time to turn a raw course prototype into a production-quality curriculum, let alone to collect a serious body of data showing how well students learn or how much schools might save.

These facts lead to a broader point. In general, the information-technology applications about which we know most are the ones that have been around the longest. Conversely, the newest Internet and Web applications have little evidence to prove, or disprove, their value for higher education. Unfortunately, these applications are the ones that, at least in theory and by logical argument, hold the most promise for confronting key challenges for higher education. So, anyone who insists on an airtight case before adopting a WWW technology will certainly be inclined to disregard, at least for now, some of the most cutting-edge ideas and applications. Digital libraries that amalgamate holdings across institutions, individual publishing ventures, cyberspace lecture halls, electronic communities of practice, and virtual universities—none of these can claim yet to be sure bets for higher education.

The question is how best to deal with this uncertainty. Plainly, an ultraconservative approach, one that accepts only proven technologies in higher education, is likely to be as irresponsible as a radical approach that embraces everything that looks appealing. In the latter case, costly errors may be committed; in the former case, valuable opportunities may be missed. In deliberating this choice, it may be instructive to reflect on lessons that businesses have learned, often painfully, in integrating information technologies into the workplace over the past 15 years.

To simplify only slightly, businesses generally have taken a very radical approach, early on adopting information technologies with relatively little forethought about which ones would best meet their needs or how they might change work practices. As a result, it has taken many years—and many billions of dollars—to demonstrate that significant productivity gains were attributable to information technology. But, finally, these gains have materialized, partly through a careful evaluation of technology options, partly because the structure of the workplace has transformed to make the best use of these new tools, and partly because productivity itself has been redefined.

What Higher Education Can Learn from Business

Higher education, now poised to take a similar plunge into information technology, can learn several lessons from these experiences. The first is that, eventually, the Internet and Web will probably live up to some of the promises offered by the examples we have reviewed. Second, it is likely that this success will materialize—slowly; that many applications that now appear to be most promising will not realize those promises; and, conversely, that some that will eventually succeed spectacularly are not even on the horizon today. Third, as we have suggested several times, many successful applications will require modest or substantial organizational change on the part of higher-education institutions.

One lesson we must *not* draw from business experiences, however, is that higher education should be willing to spend billions of dollars just to begin to see returns on investments in information technology. The resources required for such a radical strategy simply do not exist, even if traditional educational institutions had the stomach for such wild experimentation (a questionable assumption, to be sure). Nor, we argue, is this necessary. Having let business bear the brunt of being the earliest adopters, higher education can, we believe, take a less radical and less costly approach and still reap the gains. But a substantial commitment is still required (not an ultraconservative strategy), and careful planning is needed to avoid as many pitfalls as can reasonably be foreseen. The remainder of this report considers some of the pieces of such a strategy.

POLICY ISSUES BYPASSED AND THOSE DISCUSSED

Our discussion has raised, but has not resolved, dozens of important research questions and policy issues. Here we focus on just a few, selecting those that have received relatively little discussion in higher education and sidestepping a few that recently have benefited from in-depth analysis. For example, several studies outline new methods of learning and teaching afforded by information technology (more-authentic and project-based curricula, among others) and the changes in class organization, as well as teacher education, needed to realize these practices.

Instead of repeating these discussions in higher education (most educational technology research and policy work is at the K–12 level), we focus on several broader issues:

- Rather than sketch how a particular higher-education institution can increase its Internet capacity, we present an overview of the issues that confront higher education as a whole in acquiring the hardware and capacity needed to realize Web-based learning on a broad scale.
- Rather than advocate specific ideas for teacher education, we consider how universities (and schools of education) might broadly be reorganized, exploiting Internet technology to facilitate faculty learning and to encourage the creation of high-quality products for learning.
- And, rather than discuss the costs, benefits, and processes involved in realizing particular technologies (say, a virtual university), we outline the types of questions that need to be answered to select from among different technology models.

HOW WILL HIGHER EDUCATION ACQUIRE SUFFICIENT INTERNET INFRASTRUCTURE?

On the surface, possibly the greatest barrier to moving higher education onto the Internet and Web in a big way is technical feasibility. Many higher-education institutions are now developing and implementing plans for distance learning around technologies having much less functionality than the Web will shortly offer—for example, videotape sent through the mail, one-way TV (over cable channels) augmented with two-way audio (through telephones), or two-way video-conferencing using special-purpose hardware. To some of them, a proposal to use the Internet and Web for fully interactive, high-bandwidth, and multimedia courseware must look very premature. Perhaps, some will say, this is the Cadillac (if not the Mercedes) we all might be able to enjoy ten years from now, but we need to get started today—even if it means beginning with an Escort (if not a Yugo).

Is the idea of using the Internet and Web on a broad scale in higher education today very unrealistic? Is this functionality beyond the admittedly modest, if not shrinking, pocketbooks of universities and colleges? It is true that many higher-education institutions have little Web presence at this time. California's community colleges, for example, represent over 100 schools and serve more than 1.5 million students per year, but as of April 1997, some of the schools were not connected to the Internet at all.[1] Of those that *are* wired, nearly one-half provide just brief electronic brochures advertising the campus and its mission. This is certainly a long way from the ample Internet capacity education institutions will need to support richly interactive course materials and electronic learning communities.

However, in one sense, this example is looking at the glass as half empty. Higher-education institutions, in general, are very well represented on the Internet, which is hardly surprising: For its first 25 years, the Internet was inhabited mainly by universities, nonprofits, and government agencies. True, colleges and smaller universities still lag behind, but the larger schools remain among the most extensive and most sophisticated users of Internet and Web resources—even today, as commercial sites rapidly take over cyberspace. Web sites such as GNA and Athena already show that higher education can manage mid-sized, if not yet large-scale, Internet enterprises. Put most positively, the Internet is probably the only form of information technology with which higher education has more than kept pace with the business world, both in its raw capacity and its skill in creating useful products. (On a given day, the average university classroom surely logs more Web-site hits than phone calls.) In one sense, then, to realize the many uses of the Web we have reviewed, higher education needs to *preserve* its position on the Internet more than it needs to gain new ground.

However, commercialization of the Internet and Web is sometimes viewed as jeopardizing that position and as a threat to the small academic community that used to be cyberspace. Much of this concern is well-founded; today, most of the early, free-wheeling, and unregulated "electronic frontier" is long gone. One of the specific complaints against commercial expansion of the Internet, however, is that it will steal capacity, soon filling the pipes with cybercasts of

---

[1]See Web site http://www.cccco.edu/cccco/list/ccc-list.htm/ for a list of California Community College online locations.

Instant Baseball,[2] for instance, and potentially crowding out quality educational material. Maybe so, in the short run, but over the long term, commercialization actually may benefit higher education in several ways.

To begin with, capacity shortfalls triggered by huge increases in demand for Internet services are being met quickly, as providers rapidly lay down new fiber-optic cable and devise clever ways of using old physical infrastructure (copper telephone wire, cable TV, and the broadcast spectrum) to meet new needs. All of this upgrading is being driven by the commercial sector, of course, but education can benefit too. Not only will this capacity expansion mean that educational material need not be crowded out; it actually suggests that education should have even more room in which to work than in the past, and better tools to make use of that capability.

One of the reasons skeptics view the Internet as an inadequate infrastructure for distance learning is that, even in its precommercial glory days, it did not supply the bandwidth needed to deliver rich instructional material, such as two-way video, in real-time. Today, for example, viewing short (and noninteractive) video clips using a 28.8K modem and a Web browser is a painfully slow experience—enough to make educators take refuge, again, in instructional TV. Commercialization of the Web will change this. A collection of new software and hardware products—from cable modems that provide hundreds of times the capacity of old phone lines, to digital wireless connections, to fractal compression algorithms that shrink movies so that they fit comfortably on old phone lines—will permit the Internet to carry interactive multimedia courseware, including video, from education servers to most homes (those that have cable TV or home computers, at least) and businesses.

At the same time that commercial interests have expanded the capacity of the Internet, new tools, along with economies of scale, are

---

[2]Instant Baseball is an Internet site that uses a Java-animated ballfield to present, in virtual real-time, nearly every play in a major league baseball game. Instant Ballpark provides animation, lineups, the status of all current games, and personalized replay of any part of any game played during the current season. See http://www.instantsports.com/.

causing prices to drop dramatically. For example, video conferencing (in business as well as in educational settings) used to require special-purpose and costly hardware. Now it can be done equally well on the Internet, using ordinary PCs equipped with cameras (some machines come with cameras already built in) and running software tools such as CU-SeeMe. Although costs and features vary somewhat from site to site, Internet video conferencing probably costs, on average, about one-tenth the cost of special-purpose systems. (CU-SeeMe itself is free.) And this savings does not factor in the greater flexibility of Internet video conferencing: special-purpose video conferencing systems deliver instruction in only one way; networked PCs can be configured for video conferencing or for many of the other instructional models we have reviewed here.

Issues and Policies for Acquiring Internet Infrastructure

In short, then, far from threatening higher education's position, commercialization of the Web is providing the tools and capacity needed to create and deliver interactive, multimedia courseware at very low prices. But knowing this is still a long way from saying how specific institutions should go about building their Web products, how they can be guaranteed the broadest and least-expensive Internet access, or how much it might cost to wire universities and colleges. Several recent studies have offered cost estimates for wiring primary and secondary schools on the information superhighway, describing the characteristics and prices of various connectivity models. We are not aware of comparable analyses at the post-secondary level, and it is beyond the scope of this report to offer one.[3] However, we discuss a few broad issues and specific strategies that can help higher education keep Internet costs to a minimum while increasing access and functionality.

Coordinated technology plans and purchases. The simplest such strategy that higher-education institutions—actually, *all* educational

---

[3]The cost of providing Internet and Web capability to all public higher-education institutions across the country is yet another topic worthy of an in-depth analysis. Several models, differing primarily in richness of connectivity and end-user hardware, would need to be considered. To estimate costs accurately, the current levels of Internet penetration would have to be taken into account, as would the price of generating courseware and educating faculty.

institutions—should have is to change their model for technology acquisition. Today schools at all levels buy (piecemeal) hardware, infrastructure, software, and support services for computers and networking, usually through funding mechanisms that provide only small, yearly technology allocations and that rely heavily on intermittent donations from large foundations or corporations. Sometimes these windfalls enable institutions to build impressive technology-intensive centers through substantial one-time investments. But to put together broad technology infrastructures, higher education would do much better to plan technology purchases more systematically, as corporations do, and especially to coordinate acquisitions across a whole campus, institution, or even a system of schools.

Currently, telecommunication providers generally regard education as a collection of small, sporadic buyers of computing goods and services, rather than as large consumers whose purchases are driven by a well-designed technology plan. As always, big, organized buyers will get much more for their dollar than small, inconsistent ones. This is a pity, because education is actually a huge industry, but one that is handicapped because of its fragmentation. By coordinating purchases around a coherent vision, higher-education institutions would obtain much better prices; perhaps more important, they could command the kinds of personalized services that only major industries such as aerospace and entertainment now enjoy.

Exploiting a window of opportunity provided by the Telecommunications Act of 1996. As important as it is for higher education to develop long-term technology plans and form large-scale purchasing alliances in order to negotiate effectively for Internet infrastructure, taking less-direct policy actions may be even more crucial. State and federal debates are now setting the stage for regulations that will influence the quantity, quality, distribution, and cost of telecommunication infrastructure and services over the coming decades. New laws forged during these deliberations will certainly change the character of the Internet in many ways, potentially affecting educational applications just as profoundly as they do commercial applications.

The centerpiece of this legislation is the Telecommunications Act of 1996. With the act's passage, many think the best window of opportunity for influencing policy so that it will benefit education is now gone. Not so. In fact, the act ignores several critical issues, delegates some decisions, and defers yet others to later dates. A brief sampling of some of these still-open opportunities (Figure 6.1) shows that Internet capabilities available to higher education, and their costs,

Issue	*Implications for Education*
Universal Service. The act provides only broad guidelines for universal service. The real fights will take place at the state level, between the FCC and Public Utilities Commissions.	Local battles will decide what *universal service* means now, and how it evolves over time. Eventually, it could include Internet and broadband access for all. Now, it just covers phone service.
Consumer Protection. Federal and state regulatory agencies still must set rules governing competition in local phone (and often cable) markets. Long-distance companies are already fighting for a "modem tax."	These local battles will have direct effects on consumers' choices and rates. They may also affect Internet costs, which are currently low and independent of distance. Long-distance phone companies are challenging this situation.
Intellectual Property. Decisions concerning intellectual-property rights were not addressed in the act. Congress is currently holding separate hearings on them.	At stake is whether current principles of fair use and public domain will apply to electronic communications. The current administration's White Paper would make even browsing copyrighted documents an infringement.
Spectrum Auctions. Spectrum decisions were initially part of the act, but were stricken at the last minute. At issue is whether networks will be granted spectrum for free, or whether it will be auctioned by the FCC (garnering tens of billions of dollars).	If the spectrum is auctioned, proceeds could be reinvested, for example, to wire schools and fund educational services. Alternatively, if the spectrum is not auctioned, TV networks could be required to dedicate fixed amounts of bandwidth to education and training.

Figure 6.1—What the Telecommunications Act of 1996 Doesn't Tell You

could look very different, depending on the outcome of political fights still to come in Washington and state legislatures. In the best of all worlds, consumers would pay modest amounts to access courseware across the Web, regardless of distance, providers would have multiple paths along which to distribute their courseware, and both would be relatively free to use copyrighted material for learning purposes. In the worst of all worlds, consumers would pay substantial sums to access courseware at a distance, providers would enjoy few options for distributing materials, and the content produced and consumed would be severely limited by extremely tight intellectual-property laws.

Whether the world turns out closer to the best of all, or more like the worst of all, will depend, in part, on how effectively advocates argue higher education's case over the next year or two. Based on history, prospects look bleak indeed. While publishers, cable, and telephone companies have powerful lobbies in Washington, education's cause in the telecommunications-reform debates is being championed by only a few educational organizations and a handful in Congress.

When it comes to political advocacy, higher education is about as fragmented as it is in technology acquisition, and with similar results—or lack of results. However, if higher education could patch together its uncoordinated constituencies, it could achieve the size, and eventually the clout, of a powerful lobbying organization such as the American Association of Retired Persons. A group with even a fraction of that weight might help steer many ongoing telecommunications debates in favor of education. But to do so would require that different institutions unite behind a broad common vision of what they want to do in education and what technology tools are required to get the job done—to become, if necessary, a single-issue group that sends a consistent message about the telecommunications infrastructure it will need in the next century.

How Will Individual Learners Access Internet-Based Education?

Even if higher-education institutions can secure the infrastructure needed to supply generous amounts of richly interactive courseware across the Internet, only one-half of the problem is solved. The rest will be accomplished when consumers—students of all ages—are able to interact comfortably and cheaply with these products. Many already can, of course. But, if education on the Internet is to be as readily available as education in the classroom, students of all ages will need almost universal access to online courseware. Today, this is not the case.

Assuming that cable TV, upgraded phone lines, or new wireless paths can bring the Internet to the door (admittedly a somewhat open question), students still need machines on which to display, process, and even create digital courseware. Right now, the only machine that does this is a personal (or bigger) computer, which, adequately equipped for Net surfing, costs little more than $1,000—about one-half what a comparable machine cost just three years ago. Roughly one-third of U.S. households have at least one PC; however, while this number is steadily growing, the fraction is not changing very rapidly, in part because PCs remain several times more expensive than other information appliances, such as TVs. This means that the next decade, at least, will see a gap of 50 percent or more between the goal of universal access and the percentage of homes that are likely to have PCs.[4] Can this gap be completely closed, and at what cost?

Technology changes, ushered in by commercialization of the Internet, certainly will shrink the gap somewhat. PC prices will continue to drop, which, combined with increases in computer demand (in part to access Internet and Web products), will draw some consumers on board. But, the advent of dedicated Internet appliances (at perhaps $500 per unit), or possibly Web televisions (which, for much less than $1,000 allow passive TV watching as well as more-active Web browsing), is likely to more immediately increase Internet access. How much and how quickly it shrinks the universal-access gap is anyone's guess. One generous conjecture might be that, within a decade, 75 percent of households will have some kind of

---

[4]The percentage of households that have *access* to a PC, of course, will be higher than the percentage that own one; some might use computers at the office, or perhaps at public sites such as libraries. Using computer-access figures rather than numbers for computer ownership, therefore, will reduce somewhat the gaps we calculate, but not enough to change our argument significantly. Moreover, one might argue that a level of Internet access adequate for education would necessitate PC availability "anytime, anywhere," which, generally, is best achieved at home.

Internet machine—about midway between the percentages of households with cable TV (65 percent) and with VCRs (85 percent).

Given a serious commitment to universal access, policy instruments, rather than technological devices, probably will be needed to cut further into the remaining 25 percent gap. The policies that are appropriate will depend on who makes up this remainder. Many ideas have been considered: Universities could supply machines for students (some already do); older computers might be recycled to low-income students; libraries and other community services could provide Internet access; manufacturers might consider pay terminals (analogous to pay telephones); and governments could use vouchers as well as other forms of cross-subsidy.

It is beyond the scope of this report to articulate policies in detail, or to outline whom they should target. (See Anderson, Bikson, et al., 1995, for relevant analyses.) Suffice it to say that students most in need of help will have relatively low incomes and low education levels. In short, many of those who would profit most by Internet appliances will be least able to afford them.

HOW WILL HIGHER EDUCATION ACQUIRE QUALITY COURSEWARE AND EDUCATE FACULTY?

If universities and students soon enjoy lavish Internet capacity, they still will need quality Web learning products that make good use of this capacity. To judge by current offerings, obtaining such products will take a long time. As any Net surfer knows, most Web sites offer little of value, and what useful educational products do exist are difficult to find, because they are usually "hidden" in isolated pages rather than combined into well-organized structures akin to textbook chapters or libraries. Moreover, the first generation of tools for creating Web documents was far from user-friendly: Faculty who built homepages needed to be skilled word processors, understand the rudiments of HTML (the current de facto standard for Web products), have access to tools that translate files among several different text and video formats, and even program in Java, in order to develop highly interactive educational products.

In spite of these challenges, there are several reasons for optimism. First, as we have seen, Web-based courseware is already beginning to flourish, and sites such as the World Lecture Hall, GNA, and MOLI are adding several layers of organization to these individual products. In doing so, they are both facilitating access by students and making it easier for faculty to find and build new online courses. A related bonus is that courseware is becoming easier to construct, in part because much Web publishing is based on a nontraditional model for creating content: Instead of being created from scratch, new courses are often built from previous ones, using simple digital cut and paste—just one example of how the Web encourages rapid development by facilitating layering of products, one on another. Layering means that individual faculty will be able to build much courseware using just simple editing tools; not all will need to master the programming skills usually required to create courseware from scratch.

Driven by a rapidly evolving commercial market, software vendors are now coming up with a new generation of tools that will automate much of the construction of Web courseware, so that it is becoming easier to create courseware from scratch when necessary. In the past, constructing even the simplest Web homepage required at least a bit of HTML coding. Now faculty can use off-the-shelf tools to create many multimedia products with almost no direct programming. Some tools convert existing documents into Web-ready format (e.g., Sunrise Packaging's rtftohtml); others build new homepages through dialogues with users (e.g., Microsoft's FrontPage); still others provide high-level graphical interfaces, delegating the synthesis of low-level HTML code to underlying software (e.g., SoftQuad's HoTMetaL PRO). Predictably, a few Web publishing wizards have put together sites that organize many of these diverse authoring resources, providing a valuable starting point for those interested in learning about them.

Finally, and perhaps most important, online information sources and support communities abound. They will help even the least-Web-savvy faculty member develop the necessary Web and Internet skills. These sources take several forms, ranging from simple FAQs (lists of frequently asked questions, plus answers), to detailed hypertext documents on the art of HTML programming, to newsgroups and listservs that engage in active discussions on how to provide Web services. All these are free. For a fee, any of hundreds of start-up companies that now offer Web product-development support will gladly design and implement Internet sites of any size, or will assist institutions or individual faculty in doing so.[5]

Issues and Policies for Acquiring Quality Courseware and Educating Faculty

Even if all these tools and supports help faculty become comfortable creating and teaching Web-based distance-learning courses, higher-education institutions will probably need to consider several kinds of changes and policies to smooth what might be a substantial transformation for many teachers. An obvious first step might be to offer courses that give faculty hands-on training with Web publishing technologies and, more broadly, that demonstrate examples of good Web courseware and principles for creating useful educational products on the Internet. But who will provide such teacher training services? We suggest several possibilities below.

Who will teach the teachers? It is natural to expect that schools of education would continue to play a pivotal role here. Certainly they will need to revamp many programs to help faculty acquire new teaching skills that are better suited to technology-intensive classrooms—classrooms that will be less dominated by lecture and more driven by collaborative projects or online mentoring. But to delegate all training on Web publishing, as well as on new teaching practices, to schools of education might risk duplicating services unnecessarily since, as we just noted, online communities are already poised to do much of the job and offer yet another example of new electronic communities that crisscross the boundaries of traditional higher-education institutions. Higher education must find strategies for coordinating with such communities, if only because much of the literature and training they offer is good—and free.

Although courses and electronic communities might help faculty acquire skills in Web-based courseware development, one big question

[5]We do not discuss these providers in detail, in part because we assume higher education, unlike many other businesses, cannot afford to outsource such services. However, partnerships might be feasible if (as with Internet infrastructure) universities would coordinate their fragmented constituents, in effect becoming a large consumer that could command first-rate Web development services for cut-rate prices.

remains: Where will the time to acquire the skills and the money to pay for everything come from? We suggest that skills can be acquired at roughly current levels of funding, provided faculty can reallocate the time they devote to their various teaching activities. As we have noted, information technology is slowly beginning to displace some of the traditional teaching roles of faculty; students will spend more time working with smart software or watching digital lectures and less time listening to live discourses. This shift might tempt some schools to cut staff and thus reduce costs, but an alternative would be for faculty to be retained and to use their newly freed-up time to play other roles.

One role that may expand is intensive coaching, to help students learn when even rich interactive software is not enough. Or, faculty could spend more time creating courseware. Thus, one way to acquire better-quality online courseware, and to educate faculty to create and use it effectively, is simply to recommend that faculty be given more time and resources to engage in these activities. If the transition from lecture-intensive curricula to Web-based courseware is managed reasonably, this added course-development time may come at little or no increased cost to higher-education institutions. In effect, the outlay should come out of savings in direct teaching costs. (Over the long term, of course, it may also be more productive to hire new faculty whose strongest teaching skills are in courseware development rather than in lecture delivery. But that is a different policy decision.)

Nourishing grassroots publication. Higher-education institutions can also encourage the development of higher-quality Web courseware through tactics that help foster and manage the grassroots, or individual, publishing that is taking shape in online communities such as the World Lecture Hall. Universities and colleges could follow GNA's lead and provide a common infrastructure for online courses. The fact that many contributions in these databases already come from higher-education institutions suggests that, even today, universities have much courseware to be organized. Perhaps they would do even better to copy proprietary institutions, e.g., MOLI, which supply such value-added services as establishing areas and goals for new courseware, offering technical assistance to courseware developers, and furnishing quality-control standards.

Setting standards for courseware format will probably be as important in the long run as setting content standards. If faculty develop materials in diverse formats that do not interoperate, the advantages of creating new courseware using simple cut-and-paste tools diminish greatly. Lecture overheads rendered in PowerPoint, for example, do not mix easily with Adobe Photoshop representations. On the other hand, if universities encourage faculty to build online courses that adhere to emerging Web-document standards, they will be inviting the sharing of course products. One of the great strengths of the early Internet, veterans will say, is that intellectual products—software and ideas alike—were shared freely. The past was never really quite so grand, but it is true that the tradition of "freeware," "shareware," and "open systems" has been strong on the Internet, and it will probably continue to be essential, in some form, if individual publishing in higher education is to prosper.

This culture of sharing faces several threats, and higher education should keep them in mind, if not actively work to keep them in check. One, discussed in Chapter Three of this report, concerns copyright and, more generally, intellectual-property rights. Legislation now being drafted in Washington may cripple almost any sharing of materials copyrighted to publishing firms. However, individual faculty publishers (or their institutions) also should have protection for their intellectual products. Many professors (and some universities) already make substantial sums selling courseware (usually as books, but increasingly in educational software). As with big publishers, they too may be reluctant to share their materials without being compensated. As always, the challenge is to strike a balance that rewards innovation enough to keep new ideas (here, courseware) flowing while also maximizing the social benefits of those new ideas (here, the sharing and use of courseware).

Individual faculty, their institutions, and higher education as a sector have yet to work out clear policies that define a feasible balance point. These decisions are tough enough when restricted to a single college or university but take on added complexity when courseware is shared across institutions or even states, not just within them. Virtual universities, such as the World Lecture Hall and MOLI, will catalog courseware from any publisher that meets their standards (standards are nonexistent in the World Lecture Hall), regardless of location. In so doing, they recognize that one of the most powerful features of the Internet is that it encourages the free flow of ideas and course materials to any place in the country (and around the world)—an idea that most states and public universities have yet to come to terms with.

Such free flow is perhaps the biggest issue higher-education institutions will have to face in the near future. State and academy barriers are much tougher to defend against "invading" software than national barriers are to defend against, say, illegal aliens. Laws will need to be rewritten to reflect the fact that courseware that might be in college online catalogs will probably be derived from, or even wholesale copies made from, products found in other university databases. Nor should such sharing be viewed as simply bowing to the inexorable forces of network technologies that make editing and transmitting digital materials virtually effortless. If managed properly—for example, through careful quality controls and well-organized cataloguing services—the net effect of promoting such sharing can be a dramatic gain in the quality of Web-based courseware.

One cost of this freedom, of course, will be that the boundaries between different institutions may begin to blur, at least when it comes to course offerings, if not social functions and research reputations. (However, in some disciplines, inter-institution research collaboration is also increasing.) Such blurring suggests that, in the future, some universities might be more brokers of education, reminiscent of MOLI and GNA, than full-service providers.

Should all universities have course development as a central part of their educational mission? Answering this question goes well beyond understanding how higher-education institutions can help foster high-quality courseware on the Web; it touches on the deeper issues of new models of educational delivery that information technologies enable. In the next section, we briefly offer some answers.

HOW WILL HIGHER EDUCATION MAKE CHOICES ABOUT NEW DELIVERY MODELS FOR EDUCATION?

The preceding two sections address broad issues of feasibility and capacity, but not how such capabilities will be put to work. Assuming higher education has the financial, physical, and human resources necessary to use the Web and Internet, what structures or models should it adopt for delivering educational services?

No More One-Stop Shopping?

The dominant model of delivery in higher education is still one-stop shopping: A single provider offers all educational services (including course creation, course delivery, counseling, student evaluation and accreditation, deciding which course collections will lead to degrees, and, often, support for job placement) at a single location. (Consumers are expected to come to the provider, not the converse.) But this model may be challenged for dominance. New information technologies add substantially to the set of models that providers can consider. Many of the case studies we have reviewed demonstrate that some of these different delivery structures already have moved from the drawing board into practice. Broadly, these models unbundle educational services and repackage them in different ways. Some highly specialized providers offer only a few courses rather than large sequenced collections, some broker courses rather than creating them, and others create and deliver courses, but in partnership with several providers rather than solo.

While mass education, including primary and secondary schools, vocational and training institutions, and colleges and universities may be the most common formal method of learning, many of us remember taking piano or dance lessons from highly specialized providers. Although marginal in this country, intensive apprenticeships have persisted as powerful learning methods for centuries—so much so that many hope that information technologies soon will make cognitive apprenticeships feasible on a large scale. (See Figure 2.9.) And new information technologies are not the only reason different models of education delivery are beginning to flourish. Growing markets for adult-learning services require changes in traditional delivery models; consumers of on-the-job training, for example, insist on courses that are highly tailored to specific needs, rapidly changeable, and delivered at the workplace, not in the classroom.

New information technologies are supplying most of the raw materials from which delivery models that meet these demands can be fashioned. In the past, regardless of demand, it was prohibitively expensive to consider, say, creating courses for a widely scattered and relatively small group of consumers. Now distance matters little in the economics of such services. And whereas, once, only the largest corporate-training clients could expect house calls from education providers, today size counts for much less, because on-site education can be done mainly through high-bandwidth network virtual visits. Time is also less of a factor: House calls from education providers never came on demand; now educational courseware can be accessed across the Web 24 hours a day.

Processes and Products That Specialize

The idea that information technologies can (and should) radically transform processes and products seems routine in discussions of manufacturing and service industries, but the idea that the Internet might help reduce costs of courses or improve the quality of students' learning still draws doubts from thoughtful pundits such as Larry Cuban (1986), Neil Postman (1995), and Clifford Stoll (1995). But no one questions that the same tools help produce lower-priced, higher-quality cars. The view that technologies could help speed the creation of courses or help build courses tailored to specific learners seems original and offbeat, yet just-in-time manufacturing is familiar to anyone with even a passing knowledge of business. And while the idea that a monolithic education institution might be unbundled into a collection of services may sound altogether foreign, it is the industry conglomerate that sometimes looks out-of-touch with modern views that businesses often do much better by specializing, and perhaps partnering with others to develop products.

Questions in the Range of Alternative Education-Delivery Models

One way to encourage discussion of the different models of education delivery enabled by new information technologies such as the Internet and Web might be to try to systematically attempt to characterize the vast range, or space, of alternatives. However, doing so would probably be as cumbersome as trying to describe all the ways that businesses could restructure using new technologies. Instead, we limit ourselves to posing a series of questions—most stemming from the different applications of the Web and Internet we have reviewed—that summarize a wide range of ways the structure of educational services is changing to make effective use of new information technologies. We deliberately pose the questions as challenges to facets of the familiar one-stop-shopping model, not necessarily because that model is flawed, but because points in the "space" of alternatives nearby familiar models are likely to be explored, while more distant ones may go unnoticed. The list is by no means complete. We intend it as a spur to discussions of these unusual, and sometimes useful, alternatives.

Knowledge chunks: Why are courses so long? Courses in higher education usually extend across many weeks. Quarters and semesters vary in size across institutions, but not radically. And within institutions, there is little variation at all. Courses offered to corporations by external providers, on the other hand, often last no longer than a few hours and are driven by the needs of the client and requirements of the material, rather than by the conventions of the providers. One-size-fits-all courses certainly make bookkeeping easier for degree-granting institutions and probably are impossible to circumvent if classes must meet at scheduled times and places. But if students learn mainly at a distance, can choose to start a course when they wish, and can access courseware anyplace, anytime, perhaps courses of variable length, tailored to the needs of the subject (and, of course, to the needs and learning style of the student) are feasible.

Course flexibility: Why offer only a few courses per subject? Why not add to course listings in an ongoing fashion? Most universities and colleges change their course offerings slowly compared with MOLI and GNA. On the surface, increasing speed of course creation and the diversity of courseware could only help consumers, assuming value-added counseling services were available to help them select the products that best match their current level of expertise, educational goals, and learning styles. Tools that permit faculty to rapidly create new Web products certainly will help expand the range of courseware a university offers. However, MOLI and GNA enjoy even more flexibility, because they invite outside developers to develop online materials. Whether or not institutions can offer a large pool of courses, therefore, will probably depend on changes to other structural features, some of which are noted below.

Why limit class enrollment? Most university courses place caps on the number of students they will admit, and on the size of individual classes. In prestigious institutions, this often means that demand outstrips supply in ways that more market-driven service industries never see. Recent experiments at the City University of New York and long-term successes at the Open University indicate that distance-learning technologies can open up enrollment while keeping costs under control and quality reasonably high. As demand for quality adult education continues to grow, various models of "partially open" enrollment might be worth considering. A school might, for example, allow anyone to take a distance-learning course on the Web for a nominal fee, subject to the constraint that he or she access only online resources (such as lecture materials and electronic quizzes seen in courses on the World Lecture Hall). Students could also pay additional fees for more labor-intensive services, such as online tutoring and proctored exams.

Why should faculty spend more time directly delivering information rather than engaging in other functions, especially courseware development? If open or partially open enrollments become more common, the direct involvement of faculty in delivering education (e.g., through live lecture) probably will diminish, since more and more students will access recorded and interactive materials online, rather than attending classes. At the same time, other teaching functions, in particular the creation of courseware that is accessed at a distance, will become increasingly important. Models that emphasize content development over delivery will probably also change hiring practices; new faculty may need to be as skilled at multimedia publication as they are at playing "sage on the stage."

Why should universities develop courseware? Why not concentrate more on value-added management and brokering services? Perhaps some universities could do away with courseware development as well as with direct course delivery. The World Lecture Hall and the Global Network Academy suggest models of educational services in which the functions traditionally bundled together as one-stop shopping are now separated. Institutions that specialize in organizing courseware developed by others could offer several advantages to consumers: warehousing of many courses on a single subject, giving consumers a wide range of choices; offering only the best courseware, from superstar faculty, as does The Teaching Company

(Figure 2.10); or concentrating on other important value-added services, as does the Western Governors University (http://wga-internet.westgov.org/smart/vu/vu.html). Western Governors University is not planning to develop or deliver courseware, but will conduct needs assessments to determine areas in which course offerings are insufficient, provide quality-assurance and quality-assessment tools to measure student learning (and course efficacy), and establish requirements for degrees and other credentials, as well as supplying centralized services, including libraries and repositories of student records. More broadly, in such models, higher-education institutions would supply high-level management, resources, and vision; many of the specific tasks would be done by specialized providers.

Why not pool common information resources, such as libraries? Some new-models universities might unbundle services and specialize in a few key functions. However, alternative models might bundle pieces that are typically separate. For example, pooling courseware across institutions would give consumers greater freedom of choice. By the same token, it makes good sense to aggregate electronic libraries across institutions: Students lose nothing if a virtual library is "moved" off-campus and will gain access to richer collections if their library is merged with other holdings. These are just two examples of educational models that try to exploit some potential benefits of the free flow of information across institution, state, or even national boundaries.

Why not partner with for-profits as well as with other nonprofit and public providers? If higher-education institutions explore delivery models that unbundle services, they will also need to consider various alternatives for partnering with other providers—institutions that provide those services that they themselves have decided to delegate, and with whom they will need to coordinate if they still wish to offer full-service education. In particular, given that the for-profit sector (mainly high-tech corporate training) is expanding much more rapidly than is traditional higher education, various heterogeneous models that include a mix of public and private institutions will need to be considered.

Today, this country spends about as much on for-profit educational services as on public education; shortly, corporate training alone will exceed higher education in size. Thus, if higher education remains separate from these other participants in the adult-learning market, its presence will continue to diminish.

REFERENCES

Anderson, J. R., A. T. Corbett, K. Koedinger, and R. Pelletier. "Cognitive Tutors: Lessons Learned," *The Journal of the Learning Sciences*, Vol. 4, Issue 2, 1995, pp. 167–207.

Anderson, R. H., T. K. Bikson, S. A. Law, B. Mitchell, C. Kedzie, B. Keltner, C. W. Panis, J. Pliskin, and P. Srinagesh. *Universal Access to E-Mail: Feasibility and Societal Implications*, Santa Monica, Calif.: RAND, MR-650-MF, 1995.

Cuban, L. *Teachers and Machines*, New York: Teachers College Press, 1986.

Dewar, J. *The Information Age and the Printing Press: Looking Backward to See Ahead*, Santa Monica, Calif.: RAND P-8014, 1998.

Dwyer, D. "Apple Classrooms of Tomorrow: What We've Learned," *Educational Leadership*, April 1994, pp. 4–10.

Fletcher, D. "The Effectiveness and Cost of Interactive Videodisc Instruction," *Machine-Mediated Learning*, 3, 1989, pp. 361–385.

Gomez, L. M., and D. N. Gordin. "Establishing Project-Enhanced Classrooms Through Design," in D. Jonassen and G. McCalla, eds., *Proceedings of the International Conference on Computers in Education*, Charlottesville, Va.: AACE, 1996.

Hall, B.. "Return on Investment and Multimedia Training," *Multimedia Training and Internet Newsletter*, July–August 1995.

Katz, S., A. Lesgold, G. Eggan, and M. Gordin. "Modeling the Student in SHERLOCK II," *Journal of Artificial Intelligence and Education* (Special Issue on Student Modeling), Vol. 3, No. 4, 1993, pp. 495–518.

Kulik, J. A. "Meta-analytic Studies of Findings on Computer-Based Instruction," in E. L. Baker and H. F. O'Neil, eds., *Technology Assessment in Education and Training,*. Hillsdale, N.J.: LEA Publishers, 1994.

McArthur, D., and M. Lewis. "Muddy Learning: Evaluating Learning in Multi-User Computer-Based Environments," unpublished, 1996.

McEldowney, P. "Scholarly Electronic Journals—Trends and Academic Attitudes: A Research Proposal" (URL http://poe.acc.virginia.edu/~pm9k/libsci/ejs.html), 1995.

Perraton, H. "Comparative Cost of Distance Teaching in Higher Education: Scale and Quality," in G. Dhanarajan, P. K. Ip, K. S. Yuen, and C Swales, eds., *Economics of Distance Learning,* Hong Kong: Open Learning Press, 1994.

Postman, N. *The End of Education: Redefining the Value of School,* New York: Alfred A. Knopf, 1995.

Resnick, M. *Turtles, Termites, and Traffic Jams: Explorations in Massively Parallel Microworlds,* Cambridge, Mass.: MIT Press, 1994.

Rosen, S. "The Economics of Superstars," *American Economic Review,* Vol. 71, No. 5, 1981, pp. 845–858.

Rothenberg, J. "Ensuring the Longevity of Digital Documents," *Scientific American,* January 1995, pp. 24–29.

Stoll, C. *Silicon Snake Oil: Second Thoughts on the Information Highway,* New York: Doubleday Anchor Books, 1995.

Tyack, L., and L. Cuban. *Tinkering Toward Utopia,* Cambridge, Mass.: Harvard University Press, 1995.